THINKING THE PRESENT
RECENT AMERICAN ARCHITECTURE

K. MICHAEL HAYS AND CAROL BURNS
EDITORS

PRINCETON ARCHITECTURAL PRESS

Princeton Architectural Press
37 East Seventh Street
New York, NY 10003
212.995.9620
ISBN 0-910413-93-2

Printed in the United States of America
93 92 91 90 5 4 3 2
Editors: Carol Burns, K. Michael Hays
Book design: Kevin Lippert
Production editor: Clare Jacobson
Special thanks to Sheila Cohen, Scott Corbin,
Antje Fritsch, Elizabeth Short, and Ann Urban.

INTRODUCTION
RAFAEL MONEO

ALTHOUGH ARCHITECTURE GENERATES an immense amount of information today, the current scene is, in my view, neglected. Architects, drawn by the urgency of capturing the latest trend, are reluctant to attempt an analytic view of the immediate present. They prefer to view themselves as the interpreters of the *zeitgeist*, and thus act almost deterministically, uncompelled to explain the theoretical principles governing their work. Very rarely do architects support their views with theoretical reflections, and perhaps it is not necessary that they do so. But then theoreticians, historians, and critics must try to provide the understanding of the facts. In my opinion, however, theoreticians and historians seem more interested in the recent past than in the present. For better or for worse, they seem to think that they should work on more solid ground than the present affords, and thus the current scene is often ignored. Newspapers serve as vehicles for critical continuity and professionally developed writing on architecture. But curiously, architectural magazines are not producing criticism like art magazines. As a result, the work of architectural writers employed by newspapers takes a position halfway between information and opinion, leaving the ground open for a more incisive criticism.

Ours is a time, whether we like it or not, of self-consciousness. Human activity is performed today less automatically than it was in the past. We cannot play the part of the "noble savage." I would strongly encourage students, then, to base their work on a well-founded knowledge of the discipline, as this is the only way to achieve fruitful insight. To reflect on architecture is, in my opinion, an imperative mandate.

But it is also of extreme importance to examine contemporary architecture here, in the schools. The role of schools has changed quite dramatically during the last twenty years or so. Schools today are laboratories in which architectural ideas, and thus the future of the profession, are tested. That has not been the case in the past. Until recently, schools served as the means by which information about professional practice was disseminated and as the instruments for the propagation of ideas and concepts that had already been tested and experienced. The contrary seems to happen today. Now, schools are the battleground upon which ideas are submitted to serious scrutiny. Those ideas that survive are translated immediately into practice by young architects, who are promptly absorbed by the profession. I firmly believe, therefore, that if the schools were able to study openly the contemporary scene, it would be to the great benefit of the young architects we are educating today. If we neglect this aspect of their education, they will be forced to swim among the uncertain waters of today's architectural media without the necessary knowledge of the depths and whirlpools that move and agitate those waters. Because we at the GSD are aware of this recent change in the relationship between the school and the practice of the profession, we are strongly committed to bringing the discussion of current problems to the classroom. This collection of working papers is an important step in this direction.

You may ask why we start with an examination of the last twelve years of American architecture. As we planned the conference from which the essays here are drawn, the issue of the point at which to draw this line was a matter of much discussion. We know that the crises in commonly shared principles that occurred in the fifties, sixties, and even seventies had their origins as far back as the years in which modernism enjoyed its biggest success. Who would not agree that a figure such as Eero Saarinen was sowing the seeds of rebellion? But going so far back in time could mean a less sharp focus on today's architecture. And an examination of today's architecture is clearly our target.

We thought that if we wanted to consider today's architecture we should start from the recent past, from the middle seventies. Who would deny today that the consolidation of a different way of seeing the world, clearly expressed by the arts and immediately reflected in architecture, emerged in the seventies? We decided that Michael Graves's work in the second part of the seventies was probably the clearest example of these changes. In 1976–77, Graves, who had proved his talent as an interpreter of modernism through an intelligent use of cubist principles, decided that another architecture more in consonance with the atmosphere of the times was possible. As in many other spheres of knowledge, the perception of architecture as a discipline had been

under discussion since the beginning of the seventies. History was recon-
sidered. The value of traditional cities, both as efficient organisms and enjoy-
able places, was accepted. The art critics rediscovered the importance of content, thus denying that only formal issues should be considered. Graves observed these events with extreme attention. Nothing escaped him: the
teachings of Colin Rowe, the renewed interest in the beaux-arts tradition,
the enthusiasm for the always mysterious neoclassicism that so strongly
seduced his peers. Also, he loved the past, particularly Roman and vernacular
architecture that Leon Krier presented at Princeton as the only example of
"rational architecture." Should Graves be tied, for the rest of his life, to
transparencies, shears, and collisions, that were featured in such an exaggerated way in the Rockefeller House? He decided to change, and suddenly
elements of classical architecture—pediments, columns, stone, and so on—appeared in projects like the Fargo Cultural Center and the Crooks House.
Why not use the elements that everybody admired? The Portland Building
was a manifesto and with it Graves opened the door to the most recent
American architecture.

The big firms followed his path without doubt, thus accepting what Graves
had established in academia, using academia as the arbiter of fashion, the
judge to decide what the times needed. Philip Johnson's AT&T Building was
the first example of this. His early schemes for that building allow us to see
what the Graves conversion meant for him. Along with Johnson, all the big
firms seemed affected by the new trend. Architecture should be more joyful,
richer, more related to traditional values. And those who handled the most
important and costly commissions—from Skidmore, Owings & Merrill to
Kevin Roche, from I. M. Pei to Cesar Pelli—adhered to the new language.
A new firm—Kohn, Pederson, Fox—marked the high point of the new tendency. This new language unconsciously solved many of the problems raised
by professional practice. Massive and undifferentiated volumes, the product
of real estate speculation, could be masked with color and decoration.
Developers could find marketable diversity. People could find a longed-for
return to the understandable past. The beginning of the eighties coincided
with a new political mood designed to please everybody.

This collection of papers begins by acknowledging the impact of the new formal parameters forged by academia on professional practice. This was sudden
and unexpected. But once this characteristic feature of the eighties has been
examined, the essays proceed in another direction to investigate the evolution of those architects who led the previous decade of American architecture.

On one hand, we consider it absolutely necessary to examine the architecture
of Robert Venturi and Denise Scott Brown. Their contribution to the formation of recent architectural theory worldwide has been immense, and it is

mandatory, in our reflections here, to consider more specifically their influence on the American scene, particularly how much their ideas helped to create the atmosphere for the changes that occurred in the late seventies. Following from that, their work during the eighties has evolved in a valuable continuity that speaks about the strength of their convictions.

On the other hand, it is important to review the new coordinates of the group of architects, who in one way or another, gathered in the seventies around Peter Eisenman's Institute for Architecture and Urban Studies. If Venturi and Scott Brown wanted to establish contact with mainstream America, the New York Five tried to give an ideological basis to the profession and nurture the dream of an authentic modernity. Emphasizing the abstract principles of the discipline was their flag. During the late seventies and early eighties changes affected all of them in different ways. Eisenman, the most intellectual and alert of the group, tried new alliances. He turned to literary criticism, and his emphasis on architectural objectivity was transformed into a new proposition of architecture as text. This move opened the door to deconstructivist architecture, a concept that still attracts, mainly because of its intellectual allure, a large group of young architects.

By calling one topic "The Gehry Phenomenon," we declare the unexpected arrival of Frank Gehry's work on the American architectural scene. I think that his success should be seen as a reaction against the overly cultural and superficially elaborate approach of much of the architecture of the late seventies and early eighties. Gehry came from modernism, but reached his free manner by using mechanisms directly borrowed from artists, by acknowledging the presence of the context, and by dignifying ignored materials. His work appeals because of its freshness and its unbiased view. It recovers once more the best of an American manner without falling into the kind of sophisticated and constrained dependency on culture that seems to protect the work of many of his contemporaries. In a certain way I would dare to say that the presence of Gehry's architecture has *relocated* the interests of a younger generation of architects all over the country with amazing vigor.

Today's American scene seems to reflect the decentralized, or many-centered, structure of this country more than ever. It would be impossible to speak of "style" or "manner" without associating these with a specific geographical location or with a very precise socio-economic group. To map today's American architecture has been one of the goals of the conference and of this publication. I also hope that we have connected with the present picture of the profession, taking into consideration the social and ideological values that have definitively contributed to shape the practice. The reader will note that we have not changed the styles or voices of the speakers in this presentation, thus maintaining their diversity as a reflection of today's architectural production.

I firmly believe that if we want to understand the message that is emerging from today's American architecture, we first need to provide a free view of the panorama. To contribute to this description has been one of the primary goals of this conference. We have not intended, and I stress this point, to offer conclusions. We hoped, rather, to examine the current state of architecture and to contribute to the establishment of a map that describes the present situation. We have sought to identify the political, economic, technological, and aesthetic factors that interact with and affect architecture today, and to explore the ways in which architecture reacts to these parameters. If we have been successful in so doing, we are learning to determine the role of architecture in today's world, something that in my view is quite needed today. Where better to lay siege to this exploration than at an architecture school?

Let me publicly recognize the help of the people and institutions that have made this event possible. I should thank Mr. Carter Manny for the support provided by the Graham Foundation, as well as Mr. Graham Gund, a Boston architect who is always ready to respond to the needs of our school. I would also like to acknowledge the talent, dedication, and willingness of Margie Reeve, curator of exhibitions at the GSD, and Roxana Breckner, administrative assistant in the Department of Architecture, without whose help this conference would not have been possible.

MICHAEL GRAVES
BODYBUILDER?
PEGGY DEAMER

AS A WAY TO BEGIN, I feel the burden of making some profound observations about the general critical framework in which we should view the last twelve years, or about the significance of 1976 as a date initiating a new architectural era. However, this is a responsibility I shall ignore temporarily because I want to begin earlier than 1976 and because I think that the work of Michael Graves can only marginally be taken as representative of this era, even if it plays a significant role in initiating it.

As a point of departure, then, I want to recall Mario Gandelsonas's 1973 article, "On Reading Architecture," in which he makes the point that the work of both Graves and Peter Eisenman should be seen as systems of signification, albeit of two divergent sorts—Eisenman's syntactic, Graves's semantic.[1]
Today we might question whether Graves's work was ever rightfully subsumed into a linguistic critique. Gandelsonas has a difficult time establishing a definition of "semantic" that explains the difference between Graves's work and "ordinary" architecture, inasmuch as "normal" buildings, which he would exclude from this critique, refer, as do Graves's buildings, to things external to themselves. Yet the article reminds us that as early as 1973, Graves's work fell into this semantic realm of external "cultural" referents.

One cannot, in other words, suggest that the change in Graves's work around the year 1976 is the result of a newly found "religion" that suddenly allowed the conceptual use of representation and metaphor, or the appreciation of landscape, architectural history, or ritual. These are precisely the conditions that qualify Graves's early work and make it unlike that of Eisenman or the rest of the "Five."[2] Moreover, the written texts that surround Graves's work, from the earliest to the latest, are remarkably consistent in the themes that they pronounce. William La Riche introduces Graves's contribution to *Five Architects* by describing his attempt to enhance man's habitation of the landscape through the embodiment of ritualized activities[3]—a theme that Graves himself is still writing about today.

These texts describe a fundamentally utopian vision of what it means to dwell in nature and how architecture facilitates and expresses nature's significance. This conception of utopia is not dependent on "modernization" but envisions a present that is more spatial than social, more physical than political.[4] As such, it assumes the possibility not of an ideal social structure, but of an ideal place and landscape. Beyond this, I would say, it also suggests the possibility of an ideal human subject.

Much has been written concerning Graves's sensitivity to landscape and nature—to the space, we can say, of his utopia. Less has been written about his interest in the establishment and expression of the inhabitant of this space, the human subject. Less has been written, in other words, of his "humanism." Graves's written texts have demonstrated how literal this humanism is—how much, in the manner of Geoffrey Scott, it is equated with anthropocentricity.

But the earlier works, both written and built, demonstrate their own form of humanism, one that is expressed through parallel although different discourses. The first revolves around his concern for the sacred and profane realms of human dwelling and for the precincts, such as the threshold, of ritualized activity. These issues are drawn from Mircea Eliade's *The Sacred and the Profane* and supplemented by Gaston Bachelard's *The Poetics of Space* and Joseph Rykwert's *On Adam's House in Paradise*, all texts introduced to Graves by Peter Carl. Carl, the extremely erudite and well-read Princeton student who wrote the apologia to Graves's 1979 monograph and who later went on to teach with Rykwert at Cambridge, was by all accounts the central figure shaping Graves's general intellectual framework and directing it toward a phenomenological humanism.[5]

The second discourse revolves around Graves's subsumption of nature into the realm of human inhabitation, a concern shared with and influenced by Colin Rowe, himself a humanist in the Warburg tradition. Rowe, introduced to Graves by Eisenman when the two were teaching together at Princeton in the mid-sixties, shared with Graves an interest in a more human, post-Corbusian approach to urban design. Using landscape as a model for urban morphology, Rowe instituted a new awareness of perceptual and spatial determinants in the shaping of cities. While Graves began absorbing these lessons into his built work, he nevertheless ended by using nature secondhand.

In his double translation of landscape into urban form and back into landscape, Graves developed an appreciation not for nature, but for its human manipulation. In his use of Asplund's Royal Chancellary to generate the gardens to the Crooks and Plocek Houses, he clearly envisioned a kind of nature different from that of, say, J. B. Jackson or Alvar Aalto.[6] His landscape is man-made at the same time that it claims the utopian authority embedded in the name "nature."

These points—Graves's ideological consistency and his utopian humanism—allow us, in part, to distinguish between the apparent "postmodernism" of Graves's later work and the postmodernism of Venturi, Stern, or Moore. Where these three, in their various ways, make architecture that is defined by its position posterior to modernism—both modernism's style and the cultural aspirations that adhered to that style—Graves defines his later work by a significantly more complex agenda, one that eluded the modern/postmodern dichotomy. On the one hand, his utopian ideology and the subjective manner in which it is explored not only transcend this change in style, but also are intrinsically modern. Moreover, his commitment to architecture as a visual art, if not a painterly art, is in many ways a holdover from a modernism that subscribed to the belief in the artist as "hero" and the privileging of the eye. On the other hand, there is also the point, implicit in Graves's semantic architecture and his attachment to Rowe, that the work was never "modern" in its use of forms. His use of the language, from the start, was impure. The change in the work that I will describe, then, is less about the transformation from modernism to postmodernism than a change in the perceptual structure given to his humanism.

To understand the initial form of this visual structure, we can start with an examination of Graves's 1972 Gunwyn Ventures renovation. Here, as in the Benaceraff addition before it, color is used representationally—the green stair of the Gunwyn renovation represents a tree—and elements of the architecture are used metaphorically—the stair as "tree," the soffit as "cloud," and the flesh-colored frame as "body" also represent nature. There is also an expressed attempt to give three-dimensional form to the experience of transition from the realm of the sacred to the realm of the profane by dwelling on the notion of threshold. In other words, as I have indicated, this project has attributes associated with Graves's "postmodern" work. But it also demonstrates a particular scenographic approach to space making and indicates the point from which the later work departs.

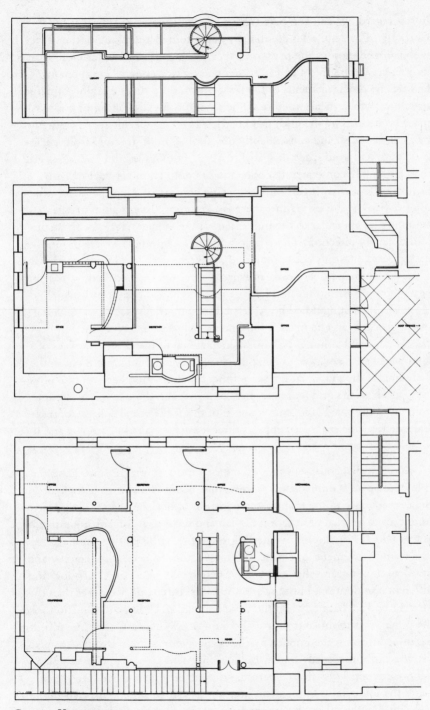

Gunwyn Ventures, 1972
(Top to bottom) third, second, and first level plans

In this regard, we can compare Graves's use of the free plan to that of Le Corbusier. For despite his continually being touted as the one of the "Five" who adhered most to the master, Graves's early work was never Corbusian in its essence. Corb's free plan can be defined by two essential components. The first are the disengagements of the facade from the structure and of horizontal structure from vertical structure.[7] The second is the distinction of universal space (as defined by the grid) from particularized or specific space (as defined by interior walls), and consequently the distinction of structure from enclosure, of object from space or spatial marker.[8] For Graves, the grid is less grid than frame. He consequently obliterates the distinction between what is horizontal and what is vertical, both being equated in a more abstract structural device. At the same time, there is a less clear "layering" of parallel spaces running perpendicular to the movement of the viewer. Here the space unfolds in every direction. There is no sense of foreground, middle ground, or background, but only the compressed manifold of the total visual field. Moreover, the distinction between "universal" space and "objectified" space disappears through various means. The use of color and curved forms, which in Corb's hands distinguished body-related (volumetric) space from universal space, becomes an end in itself for Graves, obliterating any distinction between space and volume. His murals are applied to the curved surfaces of volumes in such a way as to deny their curvature and subsume them in the flattening of the mural. At the same time, the distinction between the physical markers of the grid (column, pier, or plane) and these bodily related volumes is dissolved. The consequence of this is the visual collapse of space. Indeed, the same space that appears three-dimensionally so complex and unlimited turns shallow and lacks spatiality.[9]

Now, this spatial collapse is interesting for various formal reasons. First, the role of the plan is immediately thrown into doubt. This stems partially from the consequence of the frame—the equation of horizontal and vertical structure leads to a visual obfuscation of plan and section. As organizing principal, as that which structures movement through the building, the plan becomes irrelevant. Movement, of course, still exists; it is just bereft of hierarchy and distinctions between solids and voids. Sequential frames make each location a different composition, but they are not linked by any device other than the moving body. That body and the development of section and elevation form the principal determinants of spatial continuity. Whereas Corb's free plan still has imbedded in it the implicit axialities and symmetries of Beaux-Arts plan-making and thus visually organizes the movement sequence, Graves's plan has no sequential system to determine the subject's next move. On the one hand, the body fights to maintain position in a space striving for two-dimensionality. On the other, the emphasis on the vertical plane plays to the perceptual and sensual aspects of the viewing subject. She is being seduced at the moment that she struggles against displacement.

The plan as drawn, then, has an equally dubious status. Clearly it is the generator only in the most minimal sense of the term: it locates the position of the sectional structure, but in itself reveals nothing of the intended subjective effect. At the same time, it is the only document that gives the work both literal and phenomenological closure. As that which defines the work as an object, the plan is guaranteed its right to a painterly composition. The plan, in other words, is both less than what we normally take it to be (a mere coding of the real document) and more (it gains an independence from the vertical dimension to become its own composition). This is even more clearly shown in Graves's 1970 Drezner House plan.

Not only is the role of the plan reevaluated, but the status of the ground plane as a perceptually experienced datum changes. It loses its capacity to act as a literal or visual ground. When the viewer perceives the "scene," the horizontal plane serves virtually the same purpose as the vertical plane: both provide, as in a cubist painting, the flat field of space (the canvas) in and on which the various fragments of objects lie. Moreover, having virtually eliminated the perception of recession or depth—the z-dimension—the grounding of the remaining x- and y-axes is likewise eliminated. The scene, in other words, is not affected by gravitational force. Up could be down, just as well as back could be front, and again, the perceiver's own attachment to a ground plane becomes tangential, almost incidental.

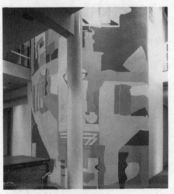 All of this confirms what in fact has become a cliche: Graves's work at this point is the three-dimensional representation of his murals, extended paintings in which plan and elevation, horizontal and vertical, figure and field are equalized as they are distributed evenly across the wall. But it is important to go beyond this point to emphasize the fact that we are witnessing not merely a visual medium (as its analogy with painting implies), but one which, in its cubism, emphasizes the act of seeing. As Gertrude Stein said of Picasso—as one can see when one has not the habit of knowing what one is looking at—it embodies "pure visibility."

The nature of this seeing subject, this "see-er," comes into focus. She not only is embodied with eyes, but eyes that simultaneously construct the context and interpret it. The creation of the context comes partially through the flattening that vision provides—vision that is naive and not influenced by what is known. It also relies on the perspectival distortion that bifocal vision engenders—the distortion that makes a horizontal plane receding in depth appear to be an angle. The abstraction resulting from this flattening and distortion plays a significant part in the possibility of reading the space metaphorically. Peter Carl, discussing Gunwyn Ventures, quotes Bachelard in saying that an individual confers metaphorical qualities upon abstractions, thus the abstract quality of the architecture allows for its poetry.[10] It is equally relevant, however, to remember Ruskin, who taught that the viewer's flattened image of the object is its own form of abstraction; it is the flattening that allows the object's symbolism to be realized.

The traditional relationship between subject and object has thus been changed. There is a conflation of their identities. Giving validity to Kant's insistence on the subject/object interdependence; to Merleau-Ponty's suggestion that since the see-er is caught up in what he sees, it is still himself he sees; and to Perez-Gomez's notion of the pre-classical or Homeric experience, which does not distinguish between the subject who sees and the object that is seen, this architecture promotes a new sense of self, one that is simultaneously defined by the inherent narcissism of the activity and the struggle to wrest one's identity away from the object.[11]

The result of this encounter is the physicality of the subjective experience. If concerns remain regarding the nature of its sensuality, rooted as it is not merely in the privileging of the eye but, one might say, in its tyranny—a tyranny questionable not merely for its narcissistic essence but also its domination at the expense of the other senses—one cannot doubt the fact that this very physicality gives substance to Graves's "humanism."

The threshold at Gunwyn Ventures exemplifies this condition. It is the plane delimiting the sacred and the profane that the real body passes through; it is also, as we have noted, an independent object identified with the human body, given its flesh-like color, its frame-like structure, and its co-positioning with the body; it symbolizes the building as a totality, in as much as the "see-er" as "seer" actively interprets the successive readings of sacred and profane, presence and absence.

The next group of projects, exemplified by the Claghorne addition of 1974 and the Crooks House of 1976, take Graves's visual sensibility one step further. If the collapse of the earlier work was phenomenal, here it is quite literal. What was previously a plane extended back into the entire depth of the building becomes bas-relief in these two projects. In Claghorne, this means not only that the volumes in the rear of the addition and the original house are legible on the front, but also that the exterior features of the house are compressed onto the vertical plane as well. The plan in this case is merely a trace, the mark left behind when the real space and the real architectural elements are compressed on the facade. This idea is given impetus when we discover that one person worked on the plan, another on the elevation, and Graves on the coloring and modulation of that elevation. Some body, in other words, chose to remain outside.

However, we are not in the presence of a nonspatial or nonvisual idea. In Claghorne, this very idea of facade and trace invokes both the eye and the interpretation of its vision. Not only do old and new become conflated, but the addition itself, like Gunwyn, redefines the meaning of threshold. In one view, the new addition can be read in its entirety as the threshold to the old house. In another, the addition, part wall and part object, depicts the various formal and conceptual qualities of threshold: the transitional plane dividing sacred and profane, respectively, as inside and outside, and the object that both locates and stands in for the body, and marks the threshold looking up, the threshold to the sky. The body feels itself consistently both in and out of the object.

I emphasize this reading of Claghorne because it is taken so often as being the break in Graves's work. It is supposedly the first time we are presented with either a facade or traditional architectural elements. To a certain extent, Claghorne does indicate a new awareness of architectural history. Supposedly, Graves went to Newport to see its Queen Anne architecture after studying Vincent Scully's *The Shingle Style and the Stick Style*. This attention to history can be understood as a visual experiment that Graves was pursuing, visiting the best of Queen Anne architecture in order to understand how to deal formally and perceptually with his own host (Queen Anne) building. The use of the lattice, while traditional, remains in the realm of pattern, one that both dematerializes the wall it is on and questions the nature of the orthogonal—the x- and y-axes. In this it is not unlike the patterned, diagonal use of tile in the earlier Alexander addition.

Nevertheless, the subject's displacement to a realm outside the actual object was set into motion in Claghorne. Other designs around this time support, if not the reading of the displaced subject, the reading of the closed facade. For example, murals no longer depict the plan nor indicate the simultaneous existence of the horizontal and vertical realm; only vertical scenes, those parallel to the visual plane, are presented.[12] And his teaching principles take a new turn at this time. In the September 1975 issue of JAE, in which he and co-author Caroline Constant explain the intentions behind his Asplund addition

studio problem, Graves both emphasizes his preference for the vertical surface over the plan and suggests that the wall might reveal its anthropomorphic essence:

> *reference [should be] made to the body image through the elements that*
> *are unique to architecture, such as walls, windows, and doors . . . The*
> *divisions made on the vertical elements are the registry of the bodily asso-*
> *ciations which cause aspects of the building's narrative to be understood.*[13]

The body, pushed out of the actual house, is now embedded in its walls.

Despite the clarification of the vertical and horizontal planes that these changes
suggest, there is another kind of tension that emerges—one that is demonstrated in the Crooks House. To a certain extent, Crooks is a continuation of
the same compressive dynamic explored at Claghorne, only in the round and
more to the extreme. All of the visual information is now lodged on the four
elevations, which can be read as the collapse of the erstwhile space behind
them. Indeed, the vertical plane is compressed even more than before; there
is no play in the facade between wall and space, inside and out; the bas-relief,
in other words, is "baser," lower, more shallow. And despite the emerging
evidence of an anthropomorphic base, middle, and top, the elevations are still

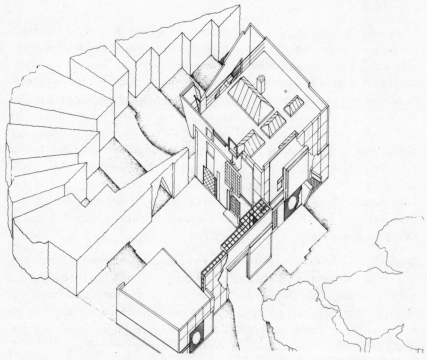

Crooks House, 1976
Axonometric

principally cubist in their defiance of gravity and conflation of the x- and y-axes, two elevations spinning around a center crossing and resisting visual focus like those of Villa Schwab. The interior plan is again the trace of the spatial contraction; it has no spatial ambiguity itself. Yet something different has happened in Crooks. The threshold, formerly the place most experientially loaded, is now flattened and encoded in the form of the keystone. Partial keystone forms reappear, lying prone in the plan. In the company of a facade that is only phenomenally constituted and a plan that is merely a trace, there is a site plan that is figural. In the place of multiple readings of inside and out, there is a single moment of anxiety when the house and garden sheer along the division line of the diptych they form. The object is in crisis.

In front of this object is a subject that, in responding to this object, is both "there" and "not there." She is "there" less because a space has been provided for her in the garden (for this is precisely the space that neither requires nor wants to be seen) than because she is witness to, if not judge of, the object's crisis.[14] She is "there" and "not there" in another sense as well, one perhaps indicative of Graves's own split personality. In the projecting wiggly plane to the left of the carport entry, one can see the silhouette of a figure that eventually emerges, full-blown, in the chimney mantel designed a year later. The line of the carport silhouette matches the line of the drawn figure to the left of the flue. Stillborn, this planar figure hints at a literal representation of the female body at the same time that it shies away from her unveiling.

It is precisely the resolution of the crisis, then, that distinguishes Fargo-Moorhead from the projects that precede it. Gone are the cubist, non-gravitational elevations, and in their stead are facades that politely distinguish bottom from top and sensibly distribute themselves laterally across the vertical plane. The plan of the building is no longer seen as a trace of the compressed space but as figural, axial, and symmetrical. The diptych remains but the moment of sheer in the form of the bridge is given spatial form and value; it is stable. And if in Crooks the notion of threshold was dizzyingly trying to establish its place, here its identity is clearly fixed. Not only are we given identifiable thresholds into the major public spaces on either side of the bridge, but the bridge itself becomes the threshold emblematized. That this threshold happens to act as a transition only between upstream and downstream reminds us that such markings, at this point, are only symbolic; they are, nevertheless, clearly constituted. Indeed, the representation of the architectural elements, particularly the keystone, is no longer obscure, even if "missing."[15]

The resolution of this crisis, however, is not without its consequences. It works at the expense of the phenomenal space it is meant to depict, for the

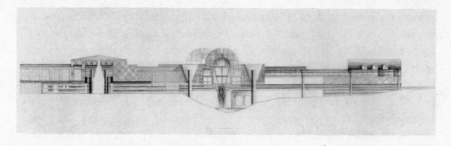

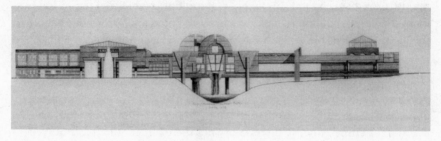

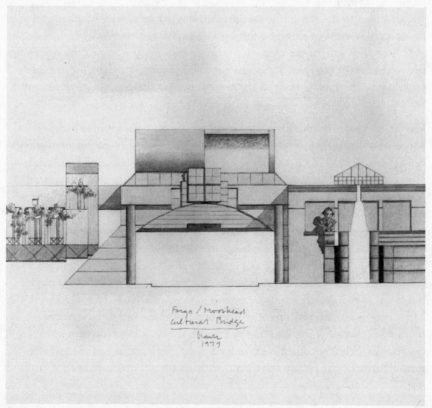

Fargo-Moorhead Cultural Center Bridge, 1977
(Top to bottom) preliminary south elevation, south elevation, detail of west elevation

resolution is coincident with the compression of the work into the plane of the paper and, with this, the removal of the sensuous subject.

The absorption of external references, wherein much of Fargo-Moorhead's appeal lies, is thus not incidental to the above-described development of Graves's work. The project's very thinness, its lack of substance, places it in the realm of the received image. If the previous exchanges were visual—between the maker, the object, and the viewing subject—the exclusion of that subject demands that the remaining interchange seek its substance elsewhere. It searches for a "look."

In this regard, Fargo-Moorhead insists that we look at influences and sources outside the rather hermetic continuum that I have been describing. Most immediately, this project reminds us that Graves was teaching at Princeton. Anthony Vidler, Graves's colleague at Princeton, provided the impetus to Platonic forms with his work on type. He also supplied the precise references for Fargo-Moorhead in his work on Ledoux, whose Salt Works at Chaux is reflected in the bridge elevation.[16] Joseph Rykwert and Dalibor Veseley also taught at Princeton for a semester in 1976, reinforcing the already entrenched phenomenological bent provided by Peter Carl. Rykwert's *On Adam's House in Paradise*, as already noted, had been part of Graves's intellectual repertoire, and the author's presence at this time surely underscored the underlying archetypal urge as well as the precise images associated with it.

Leon Krier also taught at Princeton in 1977; previously, in 1976, he had private exhibitions at the Institute for Architecture and Urban Studies and at Princeton, the latter arranged by Graves. While there was apparent antagonism between Graves and Krier when they taught together in design studio, some of Krier's images certainly were appropriated by Graves. Even if the classical tendency in Graves's work stemmed from his own interest in "humanist" architecture, the vernacular side of this classicism was signalled and supported by Krier.[17] More than Krier's images, however, his drawings themselves provided Graves with a new visual sensibility. On one level, they affected the latter's drawing style. While Graves had always used the brisk, linear ink drawing technique of Le Corbusier to study spatial organizations—perspectives, plan diagrams, and axonometrics—he now adopted Krier's more simple, cartoon-like, and flat method to examine the literally figural qualities of the facade. On another level, Krier's drawings provided an example of the successful promotion of drawings as ends in themselves.

Graves's turn toward drawn architecture was supported by other circumstances as well. It will be remembered that 1975 was the worst year of New York City's financial depression, a slump affecting both architectural practice and architectural morale. In the dearth of real commissions, a new emphasis

on architectural drawings as commodities emerged. The period of 1975–76 was
the heyday of "architecture-as-drawing" exhibitions that, despite the significant conceptual topics raised, replaced the sensuous, walking subject with
the reader of drawings: the Museum of Modern Art exhibition of March
through May 1975 and the sale at the Leo Castelli Gallery of drawings of
twenty-one American and European architects (in which Graves exhibited);
the November 1975 show at the Institute called "Goodbye Five: Work by
Young Architects," in which the majority of the projects were either drawings, paintings, photomontages, or sculptural bas-reliefs; and the inclusion in
the 1976 Venice Biennale of architects like John Hejduk, Emilio Ambasz, and
Raimund Abraham whose works were principally on paper. Most significant
of all, however, was the 1975 Beaux-Arts Exhibition at the Museum of
Modern Art, a show whose impact on the architectural community was particularly profound, not the least because it, along with other Beaux-Arts
shows demonstrating architecture's long tradition, left modernism so far behind.
For Graves, the show provided specific formal models, most particularly
Labrouste's "Pont Destine a Reunir la France a L'Italie." (Fargo-Moorhead,
you will remember, was a bridge uniting North Dakota and Minnesota
through a shared cultural institution.) But more importantly, the drawings
from the show also confirmed for Graves the seductive power of certain
works whose appeal was precisely the attention they drew to two-dimensional virtuosity.

At the same time, the Beaux-Arts show provided a method of plan-making
that at once formed a substitute for the earlier plans and filled the blank left
after the real space was compressed into a single plane. As a compositional
formula that could be used by anyone, these Beaux-Arts plans allowed
Graves to remain outside the process of their making. Likewise, they
provided a compositional method that ultimately did not interfere with his
fundamentally aspatial urge. On the one hand, he absorbed the lesson of the
Beaux-Arts composition that stressed connections and circulation over space-
making.[18] On the other, he adopted a type of space in which the real subject
need not appear. While it has been said that classical perspective separates the
subject from the object, making "the former transcendent" and "the latter
inert," it is more accurate in this case to suggest the irony of creating perspectival vanishing points into which the subject in fact disappears.[19]

Fargo Moorhead was not built, but it is interesting that in the 1982 Graves
monograph, six and one-half pages are devoted to its drawings, one and one-
half to its model. (For Portland, which was built, eight pages are devoted to
drawing, one to the model, and two to the building itself; and these two
show essentially the same view, one in color, one in black and white.) Fargo-
Moorhead is a testament to the wonders of a paper-thin architecture, not

only because it is a synthesis of known images, but because it so thoroughly understands the significance of the two-dimensional object. The drawing need not be bound by any representational demands. In this instance, not only would no one, even those in the river, get the view of the bridge that we are presented within his drawings; but the orthographic projection is misleading even on its own terms. The plan indicates that the concert hall on the left hand side of the bridge would block half the bridge elevation, but this condition is not reflected in the elevation drawing. Of course, no drawing rightly can or should represent reality. In making this disjunction neither critical nor profound, Graves uses it as a seductive ploy. The already flattened image, *vis-à-vis* the viewer, is at once more intimate than the building—one connects immediately with the attention given to the coloring lead—and more disengaged. The ease of dissemination of the drawings and the control of the process by which they are viewed depend on this separation. In this way, it is like advertisement. And like advertisement, the viewer need bring nothing to the exchange.[20]

In this regard, it is humorous to witness Vincent Scully, in his article, "Michael Graves's Allusive Architecture: The Problem of Mass," struggle with perplexity over the fact that while Graves's drawings indicate increasingly massive buildings, the actual structures never have real depth.[21] He misses the point that this thinness is built into the concept. The true products of Graves's drawings are not his buildings, but the buildings of developers who understand that these designs can be opened easily to their curtain-wall buildings.

In the final collapse of the material into the infinitely thin plane of the paper, the sensuous subject has finally been dissolved. In its stead is a substitute. The invisible audience, which has been referred to above, has neither flesh nor soul, neither presence nor duration, neither opinion nor judgement. It is a ghost. If this ghost has eyes, inasmuch as it looks at the printed image or the hung artifact, it nevertheless understands that this image has similar substance, or lack thereof. Both the subject and the object are a mirage. What the mirage holds forth is "no place," a-topos, utopia—the vision of the world that exists halfway between arcadia and wonderland, between Greece and Florida, between myth and make-believe. This is not nostalgia, it is hallucination.

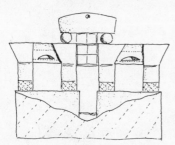

The sensual subject is displaced by its three-dimensional representation. If Gunwyn's portal was an awkward abstraction of the body and Crooks's carport threshold a quizzical reminder of the body that could not find entry into the house, Fargo-Moorhead's threshold is a clearer absorption of the body, of the human in the "humanism" of threshold.

In the early Fargo-Moorhead schemes, perhaps those that were not meant to be taken seriously, we are given the bridge as face. But in the final scheme, we are given the bust of a man resting beside the music hall threshold—a man, this time, we assume, because tradition demands the image of a Mozart or Beethoven. He is our sensuous subject who has been fossilized and encased. It is here, then, that the postmodern condition of Graves's work actually lies. The sensuous body has been replaced by its simulacrum.

I will end here, because I feel that from this project on, the work is a continuation of the reductive process that has been institutionalized by Fargo-Moorhead: the complex asymmetries become pure symmetries; the residue of the building/landscape diptych relationship becomes one of building and court; the elevations absorb their cartoon method of representation; the simple Fargo-Moorhead bust becomes the full, reclining figure of Portlandia. In all this, Graves's commitment to a utopian humanism cannot be denied. He wants, in fact, to provide us with images of a better, happier, more idyllic life. The question then is, which bodes worse for our culture? The fact that someone has this image of us or that we, for so long, have been willing to buy it?

A number of employees, colleagues, and students of Graves were interviewed for this study, and I am indebted to them for their help. The conclusions I have drawn, however, are my own and no one else should bear responsiblity for them.

1. Mario Gandelsonas, "On Reading Architecture," *Progressive Architecture* (March 1972): 69–85.

2. The "Five" refers to Michael Graves, Peter Eisenman, Charles Gwathmey, John Hejduk, and Richard Meier, the architects included in *Five Architects* (New York: Oxford University Press, 1972).

3. William La Riche, "Hanselmann House 1967: Architecture as the World Again?," *Five Architects*, 39–55.

4. See Fredric Jameson's interesting discussion of present day Utopias in his essay, "Postmodernism and Utopia," in *Utopia Post Utopia: Configurations of Nature and Culture in Recent Sculpture and Photography* (Cambridge, MA: MIT Press, 1988), 11–32.

5. *Architectural Monographs 5: Michael Graves* (New York: Rizzoli, 1979). The influence of Peter Carl (who was also reading Joyce and Freud at the time) on both Graves and the Princeton architecture school should not be underestimated. Although a student, he was older than the majority of the student body and perceived as a contemporary of Graves. After graduating, Carl worked for Graves, during which time he wrote and lectured on the architect's work. He left the office after receiving the Rome Prize. When he returned from Rome, he taught at the University of Kentucky, where he was teaching when asked to write the essay for the monograph.

6. This was pointed out to me by Alan Chimicoff, who was teaching with Graves at Princeton University at this time.

7. This of course is the point first made by Colin Rowe in his essay, "Mathematics of the Ideal Villa," *Mathematics of the Ideal Villa* (Cambridge, MA: MIT Press, 1976), 1–27.

8. This point is elaborated by Kurt Forster in "Antiquity and Modernity in the La Roche-Jeanneret Houses of 1923," *Oppositions* 15/16 (Winter/Spring 1979): 131–153.

9. See Peter Carl, "Towards a pluralist architecture," *Progressive Architecture* (February 1973), 82–88. This is an excellent analysis of the spatial intentions of Graves's architecture.

10. Ibid.

11. This reference was found in an unpublished paper by Robert McAnulty entitled "Body Troubles."

12. Heinrich Klotz, *The History of Postmodern Architecture* (Cambridge MA: MIT Press, 1988), 324-5. Klotz points out that Graves designed the murals for the New York offices of the Transammonia Corporation in 1974, at the same time, that *Oppositions*, vol. 4, reprinted Luigi Moretti's 1951 article, "Valori della Modanatura" ("The Values of Profiles"). This links Graves's murals not only to the vertical (as profile) but to the profile, in particular, of moldings and cornices and the sensuous lines they yield.

13. Michael Graves and Carroline Constant, "The Swedish Connection," *Journal of Architectural Education, Humanist Issues in Architecture*, vol. 29, no. 1 (September, 1975): 12–13. This very concise article explains how the plan, as an abstraction, is limited in its expressive

ability for its lack of physicality; only the solid, vertical surfaces have the anthropocentric and empathetic force necessary to engage the viewer. The above quotation continues:

> [Architectural] elements also have a direct relationship to our body image. When Le Corbusier in his "five points of architecture" made the window a horizontal strip, it is true that a new form was derived, but the traditional form of the window in its vertical body-related shape was lost. When the literal framing elements—head, sill, and mullions—were eliminated from the window opening, there was a consequent loss of identification relative to our bodily equilibrium.

14. The object doesn't require or want to be seen (in the sense of experiencing architecture by being inside it) because it is totally a "planometric" idea; one would be unable to understand or appreciate the "idea" from inside the space.

15. It was indicated during the discussion that this idea itself is obscure, but the point is simply that in the bridge, the structural keystone *is* missing; the one that Graves provides is a purely non-functional, symbolic one that sits below the void of its rightful position.

16. It also has been pointed out to me that Professor de Bosse was as much of an inspiration for these images as Vidler. David Coffin's course on Italian gardens also played a significant role.

17. The relationship between Krier and Graves is complex. It clearly was both a benevolent and a competitive meeting of minds sharing, at that moment, similar concerns. But despite Graves's current denial of having been influenced by Krier, both Charles Jencks and Vincent Scully, in articles that lavish praise on Graves, refer to Krier's influence on him. [Jencks, *Kings of Infinite Space* (London: St. Martins Press, 1983); Scully, "Michael Graves' Allusive Architecture: The Problem of Mass," *Michael Graves: Buildings and Projects 1966–1981* (New York: Rizzoli, 1982).]

18. There is an interesting quotation in Arthur Drexler's, *The Architecture of the Ecoles des Beaux Arts* [(Cambridge, MA: MIT Press, 1977), 114–5] by the Beaux-Arts Professor Georges Gromort:

> The role of composition pure is to link together, to make effective, to unite into a whole. It is primarily the agent of connection. It will create, in order to lead one to the various parts—to these rooms, to these libraries, to these auditoria—a whole network of vestibules, of staircases, of covered or open courts, of corridors, all of which we designate by the word circulation . . . It is the more or less graceful articulation of this network which to a great extent determines the building's appearance.

19. Hal Foster, preface to *Vision and Visuality: Dia Art Foundation Discussions in Contemporary Culture, 2* (Seattle: Bay Press, 1988).

20. For a worthwhile discussion of this topic, see Beatriz Colomina, "On Architecture, Production, and Reproduction," introduction to Revisions 2, *Architectureproduction* (New York: Princeton Architectural Press, 1988).

21. In *Michael Graves: Buildings and Projects 1966–1981*.

HIERARCHIES FOR HIRE
THE IMPACT OF THE BIG FIRMS SINCE 1976

MARTIN FILLER

THAT AMERICAN ARCHITECTURE in 1976 was poised on the threshold of enormous changes was perhaps least apparent in the work of the major corporate firms that dominated large-scale commissions and virtually defined American architecture for the rest of the world during the postwar period. Now, only a decade and a half later, the transformation of many of those firms' output has been so complete that the profound redirection of architectural values since 1976 can be gauged most tellingly by the work of a half-dozen prominent large offices. This concentration necessarily eliminates firms whose designs were essentially derivative of those six major offices, as well as those whose work is so thoroughly commercial or debased as not to merit serious analysis. This is not to say that the partnerships under discussion here are not also acutely (and often unduly) prone to following economic imperatives and stylistic trends initiated by the avant-garde. In fact, the dramatic reversal of the big offices from the form-givers of the fifties and sixties to the form-receivers of the seventies and eighties marks this period as a watershed in the transmission of architectural ideas in this country.

There is now the widespread belief that by 1976 late modernist architecture had become so drained of vitality, so denatured of meaningful extensions of the modernist design vocabulary—to say nothing of the early modernist social program—that the turn toward postmodernism (with its extensive use of ornamental motifs and allegedly more communicative symbols) was an inevitable consequence of modernism's degeneration. However, this Darwinian theory does not take into account the more expedient reasons behind the rapid adaptation to the new postmodernist fashion by so many big firms.

Most of the six offices examined here took on the protective coloration of postmodernism not so much out of philosophical conviction as from the need to offer a novel product suddenly deemed more desirable, and thus more salable, than the standard modernist offerings in a highly competitive marketplace. Whatever one might think about the quality of Michael Graves's designs or his ability to implement his eloquently expressed visions of a new architectural dispensation, there can be little doubt that his impulses are authentic and his intentions sincere. That cannot, alas, be said for many of the big firms.

The major struggle facing large architectural businesses from around 1976 onward has been that of maintaining a volume of work sufficiently lucrative to support the costly infrastructure and overhead of a large staff and physical plant; they have not been as concerned with philosophical inquiry or motivated by a genuine desire to provide more satisfactory solutions than had been the norm during the twenty-five years bracketing the resumption of large-scale building activity in the late forties and the recession of the early seventies. The tremendous strains caused by the war in Vietnam on the American economy were exacerbated by the Arab oil embargo of 1973. By 1974, the effects were already being felt in the precipitous decline both in building starts and in occupancy rates in the glut of commercial structures erected during the overly optimistic sixties. The stock market was booming and the first flush of economic activity stimulated by the Vietnam War was obscuring the burden that military fiasco would ultimately place on national prosperity. Few foresaw the wholesale dismantling of social services provided by the government or the significantly different ways in which big business would come to conduct its affairs during the eighties.

In any period of major economic upheaval there are those who respond intuitively and turn adverse conditions to their own benefit. This was certainly the case in architecture and product design during the Great Depression of the 1930s, when designers seized on the superficial styling gimmick of streamlining to make traditional styles—or even the earlier populist style of art deco—seem obsolete by contrast. As applied by the large firms, postmodernism played much the same role in the relatively lean years from 1974 to the quick acceleration of building activity that accompanied the Reagan bull market beginning in 1982. Although postmodernism was not exclusively an economically stimulated ploy, it gave an undeniable advantage to some firms—most notably Johnson/Burgee at the beginning of the period here under question, and Kohn Pedersen Fox at the end—in presenting an architectural commodity distinctively different from those of their competitors.

It must also be noted that in certain regions of the U.S., especially the Sun Belt, economic stagnation during the seventies was not as serious as it was in the North and East. Texas in particular did not experience a slowdown of building activity thanks to the immense profits reaped by the American oil industry during the Arab oil embargo and its aftermath, when artificially high petroleum prices remained in effect. It was only with the decline in oil prices during the mid- to late eighties that Texas experienced anything like the recession it missed during the midseventies.

The degree to which architectural style reflects economic conditions and social and political attitudes is often difficult to define while those forces are still in active play. It frequently takes years, often decades, before our ability to recognize and interpret those changes comes into focus. For example, it now seems clear that the rationalization of commercial architectural form typical of the big American firms during the fifties and sixties directly correlated the organizational rationalization of their corporate clients, echoing those corporations' sense of omnipotence in the American power hierarchy. Yet, coupled with that self-assurance was a certain reticence about the display of wealth, no doubt a vestige of the Great Depression, when American corporations (as well as rich individuals) knew better than to assume too ostentatious a public profile.

Such indulgences of corporate vanity as there were during the fifties and sixties tended to be internalized. When the Chase Manhattan Bank built its new headquarters in New York in 1960—the first skyscraper to rise in the Wall Street area since the Depression—the glass and steel exterior by Skidmore, Owings & Merrill was a model of modernist reticence. But the interiors were sumptuously furnished by Ward Bennett (who designed a number of pieces of furniture and tableware expressly for Chase Manhattan) while the bank's pioneering corporate art collection afforded its executives the private enjoyment of what was to become the ultimate luxury and status symbol of the two decades to come: original works of contemporary art.

By the early eighties the older belief in corporate discretion quickly began to disappear. Emboldened by the laissez-faire atmosphere created by Reaganomics and the most spectacular stock market prosperity since the twenties—as well as a pervasive endorsement of the flagrant display of wealth exhibited in all aspects of consumer behavior—the major corporate clients of the big architectural firms called for and responded to designs in which assertive forms and showy materials mimicked a hollow grandiosity and unbridled crassness reminiscent of the Gilded Age. Yet the unprecedented and escalating national deficit, the decline of the dollar as the benchmark of international currency, an alarming imbalance in international trade, and the short-term concentration on profit-taking, rather than the creation of new capital, have made it all too evident that the alleged economic boom of the past seven years has been largely illusory. Reaganomics has benefitted only a few, as the astonishing figures on the inequitable redistribution of wealth during the eighties demonstrate. Furthermore, the debilitating effect on our fundamental economic health caused by the leveraged buy out phenomenon has had the parasitic effect of draining companies of capital (either through new owners' sell-offs or through efforts to stave off takeovers) that in less rapacious times would have gone into real economic development and growth. Thus the thin veneer of prosperity papering over these dangerous indications of America's long-term economic decline has its perfect architectural analogue in the flimsy and patently superficial image presented by the vast number of large-scale works by the big firms in recent years.

Another noteworthy change since 1976 has been the reversal of roles between the big firms and the academy. During the fifties and sixties architecture schools served as feeders of young talent into a corporate mainstream that controlled the development of architectural design directions. But since 1976 the big offices have become much more susceptible to the agendas set by the architecture schools, especially those of the major East Coast institutions. The increased influence of architectural history, drawing, and theory had the effect of lessening the dominance of the large firms as sources of new ideas at the very moment when work was becoming plentiful enough to put ideas into practice. That conundrum set the tone of irresolution now typifying the production of design in the most important big partnerships that find themselves caught between a previous reputation for authority and a present tendency toward reaction.

JOHNSON/BURGEE   It is difficult to recall that in 1976 Philip Johnson occupied a much less important place on the corporate American architectural scene than he commanded a decade later. Johnson, seventy years old in 1976, was still most famous for his Glass House, the masterpiece of his Miesian style of the fifties. His precious, classicizing pastiches of the sixties (which he himself has termed his "ballet-school style") were generally regarded as a failure. It was only after teaming with John Burgee in 1967 that their firm began to move into the architectural big leagues with the large-scale, high-rise commissions Johnson had not received in twenty-five years of prior practice. Such jobs are deemed the most desirable by aspiring architects with an eye towards profits and visibility, though not necessarily quality, because of the restrictions typical of the tall building type. Johnson's claims that the late modern aesthetic was a played-out game are not borne out by his and Burgee's late modernist tall buildings of the early seventies, which showed considerably more vigor than most of their postmodernist output since. Johnson/Burgee's IDS Center of 1968–73 in Min-

neapolis and Pennzoil Place of 1972–76 in Houston demonstrate sculpturally
innovative extensions of late modernist tall building composition and act as
distinguished and unusually active components on their respective skylines.
The familiar "catch-22" of architectural patronage—requiring that one must
already have executed an example of a specific building type in order to
receive a commission—is especially strong in the case of the skyscraper.
Having built two excellent examples, Johnson/Burgee was thus perfectly
positioned to receive what turned out to be the most pivotal commission of
the past fifteen years.

It is hard to overstate the importance of the AT&T Building of 1979–84 in
New York, not so much for the thing in itself as for the decisive effect it had
on other firms that were thereby prompted to follow Johnson's audacious
break with the conventions of late modernist corporate architectural business-
as-usual. Johnson's authority as one of the chief proselytizers of the International Style was especially potent in establishing the credibility of this departure in the U.S. fifty years earlier. If the International Style became the de-
facto official mode of American big business thanks in large part to Johnson's
efforts, did not his endorsement of postmodernism predicate a similar
response from the corporate establishment upon whom the big architectural
firms have traditionally depended?

Although the chairman of AT&T specifically asked Johnson for "a building
with a top" to set it off from its flat-roofed neighbors in midtown Manhattan, not even that flouting of International Style convention was absolutely
innovative. As Hugh Stubbins's slant-roofed Citicorp Center of 1970–77 indicates, the idea was less than revolutionary. Indeed, despite AT&T's ingenious-
ly engineered skeleton (two separate towers with a veritable bridge spanning
them on each floor above the monumental, central arch of the base) this is
very much, as several critics have suggested, no more than an International
Style skyscraper dressed up in historicizing drag. Johnson's claim that AT&T
reestablished the classic tripartite formula of base, shaft, and crown decreed
for the tall building by Louis Sullivan is rendered virtually meaningless by the
fact that even some International Style skyscrapers (such as Ludwig Mies van
der Rohe's nearby Seagram Building of 1954–59) were thus organized. But at
no point in the urban setting is the entirety of the AT&T Building legible in
the way implied by Johnson/Burgee's models and drawings. Although it is
not unusual for architects's renderings to misrepresent effects of space and
light as they will actually be experienced in a finished structure, the presentation drawings for the dark and cramped street-level public spaces at AT&T
far exceed the norm in conveying the opposite of the chilling, Chiricesque
arcade.

The AT&T Building's most famous feature, the controversial split-pediment pinnacle most often likened to the top of a Chippendale highboy, is far more startling to those who have never seen the certain source for that motif— Robert Venturi's house of 1961–65 for his mother in Chestnut Hill, Pennsylvania. (The New York architectural historian Christopher Gray has recently pointed out that the 1920s Walter Steiger shoe salon on the site of the future AT&T Building was surmounted by a split-pediment top, but this seems to be no more than an interesting coincidence.) It is most ironic that Johnson, who has consistently called Venturi an important theorist but not much of a practicing architect, has used this form much as he has appropriated a great deal of Venturi's theory.

Johnson, an astute and prescient collector of contemporary art, was among the first to appreciate the importance of such central figures as Jasper Johns and Andy Warhol. Like them, he has not shrunk from appropriation as an artistic method. Yet, whereas Johns and Warhol were able to take post-Duchampian borrowings, internal references, and irony to new heights of personal expressiveness (or non-expressiveness) and penetrating cultural commentary, Johnson's cynical, opportunistic, and essentially strategic tactics have nowhere the resonance achieved by those three artists at their best. If anything, the permanence and scale of Johnson's medium as opposed to theirs seems to expose his efforts all the more cruelly. It is Johnson's failed attempt

The Crescent, 1982–85

to replicate attitudes successfully achieved by those artists that is one of the major causes of his perplexing output since AT&T.

Another source of Johnson's debased output is his flagrant abuse of historical sources based on his misreading of the essence of Karl Friedrich Schinkel's work. Johnson has cited Schinkel as a major influence since being introduced by Mies in 1930 to the Prussian master's work in Berlin. Schinkel's dazzling ability to move between the classical, Romanesque, Gothic, and utilitarian vernacular at various points in his career was not the result of casual saunterings through the pages of history books (as has been one of Johnsons's primary design techniques). Rather, it stemmed from a philosophical conviction that certain styles were more appropriate to specific building types, settings, and clients than others. Behind each of Schinkel's choices was a governing set of principles that had little to do with the random historical eclecticism of the late nineteenth century and still less to do with Johnson's grab-bag approach to the past.

Thus, Johnson/Burgee immediately followed AT&T with several more tall buildings in which different historical styles were interpreted in incongruous materials, capricious distortions of scale, and wholesale elimination of detail. The Pittsburgh Plate Glass Co. headquarters of 1979–84 derives from Sir Charles Barry's Victoria Tower of the Palace of Westminster in London of 1840–65, but its bizarre cladding in mirror glass (an advertisement for one of the firm's products) and its street-level spaces of exceptional urban insensitivity put it in a category of architectural kitsch reminiscent of the work of Minoru Yamasaki during the early sixties. The Republic Bank Center of 1981–84 in Houston does much the same with the Netherlandish-Renaissance-gable style and red granite, and again the explosion in scale and disquieting play with proportions transform the humanistic aspects of the architectural prototype into yet another exercise in urban anomie, no more preferable in the end than the worst late modernism. As is often the case in Johnson/Burgee's work, the interiors of the Republic Bank bear little relation to the exterior, and draw upon a fund of classical images that seem at first to respect human scale, but, upon further examination, serve to diminish it.

Unquestionably the most pernicious scheme produced by Johnson/Burgee since 1976 is the University of Houston School of Architecture of 1983–85. Based on Claude-Nicolas Ledoux's unbuilt House of Education of 1773–79 for Chaux, Johnson/Burgee's scandalously bastardized version takes a number of liberties with the original for reasons of economy. For example, Ledoux's podium is eliminated, the central drum of columns on the roof is squared off, and the arcade flanking the main entrance is omitted. Making this building more faithful to its model would not, however, have made it more acceptable as a place in which to teach architectural values to students in the heartland of America. Yet its particular grossness of materials and haphazard attention to detailing—as well as the thoroughly affectless aspect of the Johnson/Burgee's design as a whole—mark this as one of that firm's most contemptuous and therefore most revealing works.

For their important corporate clients, Johnson/Burgee have been more careful in recent years not to overstep the bounds of an expected propriety. As the emergence of such highly competitive new firms as Kohn Pedersen Fox began to cut heavily into their clientele, Johnson/Burgee became more mindful of the fact that although they themselves had established the stylistic definition of the postmodern corporate skyscraper, they now had rivals fully capable of getting the commissions they once virtually monopolized. Their IBM Tower of 1985–87 in Atlanta marks a step back toward a more cautious, 1920s-style conservatism. The substantial materials and regular handling of fenestration at IBM give it an undeniably dignified air, albeit an image strangely at odds with the high-tech products manufactured by the client.

On occasion, however, Johnson/Burgee is capable of producing such successful works as the Transco Tower of 1979–85 in Houston. It makes one wonder about the principals's ability to assess their own output as well as their tendency to move off into dubious stylistic directions instead of exploring the more promising realms. Though poorly received by the press, Johnson/Burgee's oval-plan 53rd at Third building of 1983–85 in New York (commonly known as the Lipstick Building) is nonetheless an interesting attempt to give a dynamic form to the usually orthogonal skyscraper. It would have worked much better had the lively, Mendelsohnian forms not been sabotaged by flashy cladding and the poorly resolved detailing of the base.

Though the volume of work in the Johnson/Burgee office (now called John Burgee Architects) is lighter than it was earlier in the eighties, one major work still on their boards is the Times Square Center, begun in 1983. This behemoth multi-tower complex, recently redesigned from the original postmodern-mansard scheme to a new, and equally poor, deconstructivist version, will irreversibly change the open nature of New York's most famous and potentially exciting urban spaces. The Great Ironist's parting shot to the city in which he created one of his most humane spaces—the Museum of Modern Art Garden of 1953—might well be this crushing, lifeless gesture at the end of a long, fascinating, but ultimately troubling career.

SKIDMORE, OWINGS & MERRILL

If one big firm could be said to perfectly exemplify corporate architectural practice during the post-war period it would be Skidmore, Owings & Merrill. Its early championing of

the International Style in the 1930s (and its canny popularization of it with
several pavilions at the 1939 New York World's Fair) brought the firm pre-
eminence during the fifties and sixties. Announced by such prophetic works
as Gordon Bunshaft's Lever House of 1950–52 in New York, its supremacy
was reconfirmed by masterful variations on the International Style skyscraper
such as Fazlur Kahn's Sears Tower of 1970–74 in Chicago. Not so much a big
firm as a veritable architectural conglomerate, SOM has three major offices—
in New York, Chicago, and San Francisco. Each branch offers a somewhat
different regional version of the house style but are nonetheless united by a
uniformly high standard of programmatic conception, materials, and detailing. This degree of intramural diversity, uncommon among the big firms
during the fifties and sixties, anticipated the pluralistic approach adopted by
many of the other large architectural offices after 1976. But SOM did not exploit this inherent advantage to maintain its position of the market leadership
it enjoyed during the firm's glory years between 1950 and 1975.

In recent years, some of the most satisfying work by SOM has emanated
from its San Francisco office, including two speculative office buildings of
1986 in that city, 388 Market Street and 88 Kearny Street. The crisply detailed
88 Kearny Street captures the feeling of the best small office buildings that
rose in San Francisco after the 1906 earthquake, with an interesting corner tur-
ret and ample expanses of windows. And yet, even at twenty stories, it does

88 Kearney Street, 1986

(left) Texas Commerce Tower, 1987;
(right) LTV Center, 1985

not contribute to the unfortunate Manhattanization of San Francisco like some other less laudable SOM designs in that city, such as the large and ungainly forty-two-story California Center of 1986.

Elsewhere in the U.S., SOM has made its mark with tall buildings that speak neither of a particularly identifiable originality of design or the kind of impressive logic that informed even the firm's less inspired efforts of the fifties and sixties. Two towers in Dallas—the LTV Center of 1985 and the Texas Commerce Tower of 1987—illustrate this change in architectural character. The LTV Center might well have been designed by any number of firms during the mid-eighties, and indeed both Cesar Pelli and Kohn Pedersen Fox have done high rises to which this bears a pronounced resemblance. If the point of this unexciting, derivative work was to achieve a greater variety and higher quality than the formulaic late modernist skyscraper, that was a misplaced expectation. The LTV Center is nonetheless preferable in its ordinariness to the flashy but shallow styling tricks of the Texas Commerce Tower, with its peel-away-masonry effect near the top of the structure, reminiscent of Cesar Pelli's World Financial Center at Battery Park City. The Texas Commerce Tower is further cheapened by the silly gimmick of a large void close to the building's pinnacle, recalling the clever high rises of the Miami firm Arquitectonica, while the curving split pediment above the void quotes the central device of Michael Graves's unexecuted Fargo-Moorehead Cultural Center of 1977.

Two schemes by SOM on the East Coast demonstrate a surprising tendency toward finicky composition, focused around a seeming anxiety over how to provide novel tops for tall buildings. SOM's entry in the South Ferry competition of 1985 for Lower Manhattan uses a spherical form at its apex much like that of the old Paramount Building on New York's Times Square. SOM's Goodwin Square of 1987 in Hartford, Connecticut, employs vaguely colonial forms stacked atop a banal base, a composition that seems sadly wanting and amateurish within sight of Richard Upjohn's magnificent dome of the Connecticut State Capitol.

The most widely praised SOM scheme of the eighties has been Boston's Rowes Wharf, by Adrian Smith of the Chicago office, completed in 1987. Its monumental central arch, surmounted by a shallow dome recalling both federal style and American Beaux-Arts style public buildings, has an undeniable popular appeal as an urban set-piece on its highly exposed waterfront site. Yet the scale of the whole complex also brings to mind the most bombastic imperialist concoctions of the last turn of the century. The classicizing Roman revival rotunda beneath the dome is similarly grandiose and retrograde, although detailing at the street level of this superblock is not nearly so overbearing and indeed in parts is admirably humane.

SOM's 1986 design for an addition to the 1920s Builders Building in Chicago is emblematic of the firm's willingness to take a more recessive stance than some of its competitors. The designers were so intent to have it blend in with the original that only prolonged scrutiny reveals one-third of the overall structure is an expansion. This can be viewed either as contextualism to a fault, or as a tribute to Chicago's City Beautiful vision of the city of harmonious symmetries rather than the city of big shoulders. SOM's largest recent work, occupying an entire city block, is Worldwide Plaza of 1987–89 in New York. It was located between Eighth and Ninth Avenues and between West 49th and 50th Streets as part of an intelligent municipal effort (aided by tax incentives) to redistribute new high-rise construction more evenly around midtown, and because of the virtual disappearance of large tall-building sites on the East Side between 34th and 59th Streets. The still predominantly low-rise West Side is far less densely developed than the East Side of Midtown, yet in one fell swoop this heretofore open neighborhood has been overbuilt by a single Brobdingnagian structure. Worldwide Plaza is a massive, squat, and overwhelmingly graceless monolith that shows that nothing at all has been learned from the mistakes of the East Side.

Nine blocks directly uptown, a newly revised scheme by David Childs of the New York office of SOM for Columbus Circle, won from the city by real estate developer Mortimer Zuckerman, is yet another example of insensitive and ill-considered overbuilding. Replacing an earlier proposed design prepared for Zuckerman by the Canadian architect Moshe Safdie (withdrawn because of intense opposition from environmentalists and the community) the two Childs schemes—an art deco-inspired, twin-tower composition and its slightly smaller second version—indicate that SOM, like most of its rival firms, never questions the basic premises of developers. All three of Zuckerman's projects are incompatible with even elementary considerations of size and scale in an urban setting directly across from Central Park. Even in a city as historically receptive to skyscrapers as New York, limits of the acceptable, not just by greedy developers but also by those large firms that willingly participate in these irrevocable acts against the quality of urban life, now are under constant attack.

CESAR PELLI AND ASSOCIATES

In 1976 Cesar Pelli was still a partner in the Los Angeles firm of Gruen Associates. At Gruen, Pelli expanded his reputation for executing dazzling, slick-tech glass-skinned buildings; his blue glass Pacific Design Center 1971–75 in West Hollywood, California is a superb and provocative example. It rises above the commercial kitsch of its surroundings with all the grandeur implied by its nickname, the Blue Whale.

Its public interior spaces are no less imposing and it remains one of the best examples of the indoor shopping mall.

In 1977, Pelli set up his own practice to which high-rise commissions, including the Four Leaf Towers of 1979–82 in Houston, came relatively quickly. Working within the same technical range as his career-making glass-skinned late modern schemes of the early seventies, Pelli began to experiment with variations of color and pattern on the glass curtain walls of the Four Leaf Towers as a means of adding more visual interest.

Pelli adopted that same colored-glass panel device for his Museum Tower and expansion of New York's Museum of Modern Art in 1980–84. The architect was obviously inspired by such early modern New York high rises as Raymond Hood's McGraw-Hill Building of 1928–30. But whereas Hood employed the colored glazed-brick cladding of his structure as a strong compositional framing device, Pelli relied on contrasting panes of glass throughout the intricately mullioned surface of the Museum Tower to create a much weaker impact. The Pelli firm's ravishing preparatory sketches of the tower— drawn by Diana Balmori, Pelli's wife—promised elevations of extraordinary subtlety, but as has often been learned since the revival of architectural drawing after 1976, drawings are not architecture and ought not to be seen as architecture's substitute or direct equivalent. The Museum Tower, for all of Pelli's manipulations of surface, is flat and undistinguished, barely any different from the average speculative office buildings that surround it. The glass-enclosed Garden Court of the Pelli Museum addition, which along with the Tower and new galleries consumed a full third of MoMA's beloved sculpture garden, draws upon the imagery of galleria-style shopping malls. Its cascade of escalators within a glitzy, grossly detailed shed are tacked onto the back of the Museum's landmark 1939 International Style building by Edward Durrell Stone and Philip Goodwin.

Pelli's much-heralded contribution to New York's Battery Park City—his World Financial Center of 1982–87, with his signature motif of peel-away masonry—has been widely influential in the work of the other big firms during the eighties. Yet the dull fenestration in both the masonry and glass walls of the World Financial Center towers, which are still certainly better than most commercial office buildings of the period, lessens the interest of this design. The dramatic, though incongruous, grove of Washingtonia palms under glass in the World Financial Center's atrium concourse adds a note of tropical fantasy to this complex.

Indiana Tower, 1983

One of Pelli's most unexpected and regrettably unexecuted schemes from this period is the Indiana Tower proposal of 1983. Intended for Indianapolis, this Bogardus-like structure resembles a nineteenth-century fire tower stretched to a vertiginous but elegant extreme.

The Norwest Center, completed in Minneapolis in 1988, indicates Pelli's return to Raymond Hood as a source of inspiration, specifically to his RCA Building of 1932–34 at Rockefeller Center in New York. Pelli's use of vertical masonry ribs rather than the horizontally striped glass panels of his designs of the early eighties gives a much firmer and more unified appearance, even as the uncommonly large windows still impart the surface sheen that Pelli generally handles so well. The principal public interior at Norwest, however, is yet another of the pompous Roman revival rotundas that have become a particular corporate cliche of this decade.

Pelli's tower for a narrow site next to New York's Carnegie Hall will add a final note of impossible congestion to West 56th Street, between Sixth and Seventh Avenues, already darkened by the midblock behemoths of the Metropolitan Tower and the Cityspire. Once again the irresistible high-rise commission meets the immovable skyscraper, and as usual it is the city that loses in this expedient alliance between a real estate developer and an architect. The former might not be expected to consider the detrimental results of such unprincipled overbuilding, but in this design, Pelli puts himself on the same level as his most opportunistic peers in a period when many architects seem unable to say no to deals of an almost Faustian magnitude.

KEVIN ROCHE, JOHN DINKELOO AND ASSOCIATES

Beginning as the successor firm to Eero Saarinen following his untimely death in 1961, Kevin Roche, John Dinkeloo and Associates did not initially follow Saarinen's tendency to strike off in a different architectural direction with virtually every new commission. Their United Nations Plaza of 1975 and its matching addition of 1983 were the firm's final essays in modernist minimalism before turning to a

different aesthetic with origins in their own brutalist phase of the sixties. Roche/
Dinkeloo has made a specialty of corporate headquarters, particularly in sub-urban settings, such as their Union Carbide headquarters completed in 1982 in Danbury, Connecticut. Like a gigantic piece of cogged machinery stretched over a bucolic landscape, this sprawling complex is entered via a road that runs directly into it and then back out, like a corporate Roadtown on the way from and to somewhere else.

Also completed in 1982, but dramatically different from Union Carbide's amorphous exterior image, is Roche/Dinkeloo's astoundingly self-important General Foods headquarters in Rye, New York. Like the domed and winged capitol building of some upstart republic, this overweening showpiece of cor-porate egotism might indeed be the perfect symbol of the new multinational business powers. In any case, it sufficiently impressed the French construction and engineering firm Bouygues (which carried out I.M. Pei & Partners' Grand Louvre designs) for them to commission a similar version for their own world headquarters outside Paris, completed in 1982. While General Foods is emphatically symmetrical, the reiteration and extension of mirror-image elements at the Bouygues Building give it a relentless obsessiveness in the great French baroque tradition.

By comparison to the pomposity of General Foods and Bouygues the vast Conoco Petroleum headquarters of 1984 in Houston is virtually relaxed. Set

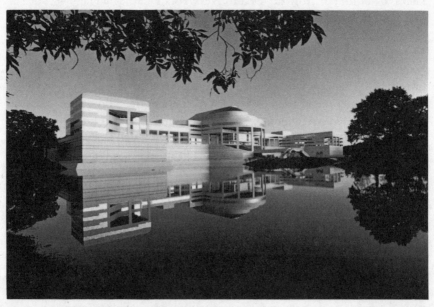

General Foods Headquarters, 1982

amidst large artificial lakes and shaded by deep, overhanging roofs, Conoco provides a suitable regional response to the realities of the Texas climate. In New York, the E.F. Hutton headquarters, completed in 1986, five years after John Dinkeloo's sudden death, was clearly influenced by Johnson/Burgee's AT&T Building, especially in its similar pink granite cladding and colossal order of columns at the street level. E.F. Hutton's negative coining of dark-tinted glass undermines the purpose of the heavy surfacing material and draws attention to the load-bearing function of the structure's steel skeleton, even as the granite attempts the contrary. This is a contradictory building without the leavening quality of complexity. The same column and capital motifs used at E.F. Hutton are much more agreeably adapted to the small, human scale pergolas of the new Central Park Zoo in New York, completed in 1988. Also in New York, across East 44th Street from Roche/Dinkeloo's United Nations Plaza, is the firm's UNICEF headquarters of 1988. This medium-rise structure, with its stripes and mansard roofs, would be quite at home in the Beaux Arts influenced commercial office section of Northwest Washington, D. C. But it is not very convincing in the more varied Manhattan streetscape, even though its lively coloration is a welcome contrast to the typical gray New York monotone. Roche/Dinkeloo's 1989 design for the Chicago headquarters of the Leo Burnett Co. is noteworthy for its flat top, perhaps presaging a return to a form that for most of the preceding decade was as much of a taboo as the pitched roof had been during the heyday of the International Style.

I.M. PEI & PARTNERS

I.M. Pei & Partners (now called Pei Cobb Freed & Partners) was archetypal among those big firms that by the late seventies had nothing to gain and everything to lose from a redefinition of the stylistic terms of mainstream architectural practice. One of the firm's longest running commissions was the John Fitzgerald Kennedy Memorial Library, which it won in the late sixties. The first Kennedy Library scheme was a truncated glass pyramid to be erected on a site adjacent to Harvard Square in Cambridge, Massachusetts. After strenuous community opposition the project was moved to a remote point of land in Boston Harbor, where a revised scheme was completed in 1979. Suburban corporate office buildings, such as one for IBM in Purchase, New York, completed in 1984, epitomize the Pei firm's suave balancing act between discreet image-making and rationalized play with geometric sculptural form (I.M. Pei's personal interest and primary *leitmotif* throughout his career). Pei's immense prestige on the international scene, which, if anything, exceeds his stature in the U.S., has led his office to a significant amount of foreign work, none more sym-

Fragrant Hill Hotel, 1981–82

bolically evocative than the Fragrant Hill Hotel of 1981–82 near Beijing in
China, the country of Pei's birth. His use of traditional Chinese decorative
motifs showed a new willingness to depart from his usual stark surfaces
when the occasion called for it. The hotel's atrium, covered by a glass-
enclosed space frame
(a motif often seen in the Pei firm's work) is most often associated with
designs by another of the principals of I.M. Pei & Partners, James Ingo
Freed.

Freed's Jacob K. Javits Convention Center in New York, completed in 1986,
contains a magnificent main interior court that is one of the most spectacular
examples of glass and metal space-frame architecture to be seen in recent
years, although the mute reflective glass exterior of this sprawling scheme
leaves a great deal to be desired. A very different direction has been pursued
by another of the Pei partners, Henry Cobb. His Portland Museum in Maine
owes a significant debt to Louis Kahn, while his National Gallery addition
scheme for London is even more explicit in its historicizing references, this
time to John Nash and to regency architecture in general. Cobb's latter
design would have been inconceivable had it come from the Pei office a
decade earlier. Now, however, it seems thoroughly acceptable to an office
that has encouraged individual partners to pursue their separate directions
rather than hew to a strict house style (as was common among the big firms
of the fifties and sixties). It is very clear that at the Pei office the current mul-

Jacob K. Javits Convention Center, 1986

tiplicity of approaches is not a marketing ploy or a commercial accommodation, but rather the reflection of genuine convictions arrived at after long (and no doubt occasionally painful) deliberation. This is not architecture-of-the-month.

The London National Gallery scheme is by no means typical of the extensive museum commissions the Pei firm received in the wake of its highly praised East Building of the National Gallery of Art completed in 1978 in Washington, D.C. Far more characteristic is their 1982 addition to the Boston Museum of Fine Arts. Unfortunately, the predominant imagery of both the blank, inward-turning exterior and the extensive non-gallery areas of the interior is yet again that of the suburban shopping mall, perhaps unintentionally apt for the mass consumer experience that museum-going has become in the 1980s.

The Grand Louvre in Paris, whose first phase was completed in 1989, is fortunately free of those commercial overtones. The Louvre's controversial glass pyramid—which began in somewhat different form in Cambridge—can at last be appreciated as only the tip of an iceberg embracing the reorganization and expansion of the historic museum. Exceptionally well worked out, this initial installment of the overall plan, to be completed for the Louvre's bicentennial in 1993, bodes well for the resolution of the entire scheme. For now, the magnificent new plaza facing the Tuileries Gardens and the majestic space beneath the already-famous pyramid make the Grand Louvre unquestionably the grandest of François Mitterand's Grands Projets. Recently, the Pei office has shifted its primary focus from the large-scale commercial jobs that sustained the office during its growth decade of the seventies to more prestigious projects with higher cultural connotations, such as museums and concert halls. I.M. Pei expressed concern over his (and his firm's) lasting reputation, and he is now more interested in commissions that will enhance his stature than those that will merely add more income.

Completed in 1989 is the new Bank of China in Hong Kong, a highly abstract, high-tech tower rising above a historicizing masonry base. Those contrasting messages within a single design sum up a moment of transition in a firm that has handled change with more grace than many of its competitors since 1976.

KOHN PEDERSEN FOX

Ameritrust Center, 1988

No big firm that has emerged on the American scene since 1976 has been more paradigmatic of general developments than Kohn Pedersen Fox, which was founded that year. Whereas in the early eighties it seemed as though Johnson/Burgee had a major project underway in virtually every major American city, that now appears to be the case with KPF. But their position seems particularly significant not so much because of their volume of work but because of the diversity of aesthetic gambits they are willing to employ in order to get the big commissions. Although William Pedersen recently averred that "the internal competition among the design participants has been beneficial to the design environment within the office," that openly contentious atmosphere could be a major contributing factor behind the bewilderingly mutable output of KPF.

The hugely successful 333 Wacker Drive Building of 1981–83 in Chicago by Pedersen spurred repeated requests by clients for similar work. But the firm's quest for novelty took precedence over a more traditional research into the resolution of design problems (even though Pedersen has explained the diverse look of KPF designs as resulting from the responsive reaction to the greatly varying conditions behind each commission). KPF partner Arthur May's 8 Penn Center building of 1982 in Philadelphia continued the taut glass skin motif of 333 Wacker Drive, but a masonry side elevation of his Hercules, Inc. headquarters building in Wilmington, Delaware hints at more dramatic juxtapositions by May a year later.

Pedersen's twin-towered Proctor & Gamble headquarters of 1984–88 in Cincinnati has been KPF's most admired project, a strong urban presence in a city whose economy the client largely dominates. The public interiors, however, imply a sense of control that verges on the menacing, a rigid and inflexible formality with slight echoes of art deco design but without the ingratiating charm of that popular style. A far better example of a cooperative urban identity is May's best design, the Four Seasons Hotel of 1982 in Philadelphia. This is a fine example of architecture that is at once substantial and yet self-effacing, respectful of the Beaux Arts configuration of Logan Circle but far from neutral in its civic impact. The new contextualism has rarely been executed with greater tact in an American urban setting during a period of *laissez-faire* planning attitudes.

In its eagerness to be everything to all clients, KPF can often be shamelessly derivative, as is the case with Robert Evan's CNG Tower of 1987 in Pittsburgh, a postmodern classical high rise that is more Gravesian than Graves. At the other extreme is the recessiveness of Pedersen's 101 Federal Street Building of 1984 in Boston, a "background" building reminiscent not of any contemporary high-style tendencies but of average 1920s commercial office construction, such as E. R. Graham's Equitable Life Insurance Building of 1913–15 in New York. In New York, KPF's work has been extensive in number and in aesthetic range, including Arthur May's widely touted but in fact highly compromised apartment building of 1986 at 180 East 70th Street, Robert Evans's excellent ABC Phase II Building of 1986, and Evans's equally pleasing ABC Studios 23/24 of 1984, a rare example of a first-rate industrial building by one of the big firms, which now usually shun such utilitarian jobs.

Pedersen has called his 70 East 55th Street Building of 1984-87 the extreme to which he is willing to take the classical vocabulary in his architecture, but his 383 Madison Avenue Tower, begun in 1989, seems in several respects like a megalithic inflation of the former. Pedersen's gray granite-clad 135 East 57th Street Building has garnered praise for its concave facade and plaza within the space inscribed by that arc. However, as with the exhibitionistic, set-back plazas that proliferated in New York during the late fifties and sixties, such attention-getting devices can have a destructive effect on the coherence of the street wall, one of Manhattan's most important compositional constants. Most promising of all of Pedersen's—and indeed KPF's—recent designs is the proposed Rockefeller Center West Tower of 1988. A respectful homage to the great ensemble of Rockefeller Center to the east and to Times Square on the south and west, this clean-lined, thirties-inspired slab will be enlivened with an enormous electronic billboard facing the famous honky-tonk crossroads of New York. It shows the firm's often uncontrolled exuberance channeled into a more constructive urban participation than has often been the case in its large but extraordinarily uneven output. The future development of the ultimate careerist architectural firm of the eighties will be watched with all the close attention customarily devoted to those phenomena perfectly expressive of their moments in history.

CONCLUSION   As we have seen in the works of these six big firms, the large architectural offices, once esteemed as bastions of predictability and consistency, have become particularly prone to a variety of stylistic modes: not just sequentially, as has often occurred in the past, but simultaneously, a particularly eighties phenomenon. The reasons for this pluralism differ greatly in each case, ranging from the capricious historical flâneurism of Philip Johnson, to the divergent interests of the principals in the Pei office, to the market-oriented improvisations of Kohn Pedersen Fox, to the seeming confusion following four decades of extraordinary modernist orthodoxy at Skidmore, Owings & Merrill. Furthermore, the speed with which some of those firms acceded to the pressure to embrace postmodernism within the first few years of its extraordinarily well-publicized arrival in the late seventies indicates that they could just as well reverse direction now that postmodernism seems to be on the wane as an architectural fashion. Furthermore, the evidence of a new interest in modernism emerging from architecture schools today supports the growing perception shared by many observers that post-modernism was by no means the epochal development its propagandists claimed it to be a decade ago. In fact, it might turn out to be a short-lived substyle that will nonetheless leave its mark because of the historical coincidence of its symbolic suitability at a time of political and social conservatism and a concurrent period of intense building activity.

Those of us who believe in architecture as the all-revealing mirror of a society's values have had to endure, since 1976, such commentators as Philip Johnson repeatedly trumpeting his pride in being a "whore," Robert A.M. Stern swooning over the revivalist architecture of the Gilded Age to excite the conspicuous consumers of the Second Gilded Age in his television series *Pride of Place*, and Tom Wolfe spewing forth his xenophobic, error-ridden, reactionary view of twentieth-century architecture in *From Bauhaus to Our House*, the period's best-selling popular book on an architectural theme. It is impossible not to see these comments as an inherent part of the political conservatism that so drastically altered the American social contract after the 1980 presidential election. The kind of architecture promoted by Johnson, Stern, and Wolfe is its even more substantial embodiment.

We have been cautioned by those who resist such social and political interpretations that even the Medicis, an unusually scheming and occasionally bloodthirsty lot, could produce architecture of extreme beauty and civic benefit (though their will to overwhelm seems fully evident in those other-wise harmonious compositions). Thus the predominant public values of the Age of Reagan have found their reflected image in our architecture—nostalgia for a simpler though illusory past, a thirst for recapturing the earlier international stature of America at the very time it was losing its economic predominance on the world stage, the evasion of social welfare issues, and the endorsement of greed to an extent never before openly admitted in our country's history.

Some of the big firms discussed here have been active agents in this process. Others have been passive conduits, tending to receive the lion's share of big corporate commissions. And even when a maverick innovator such as Frank Gehry is given the rare opportunity to design a large-scale project for a major real estate developer, such as the now-abandoned Madison Square Garden redevelopment scheme sponsored by Olympia & York, he—and of course almost never *she*—is inevitably paired with an architect from a big mainstream firm. In the case of Madison Square Garden, the architectural shotgun marriage between Gehry and David Childs of SOM resulted in one of the most uncharacteristically listless designs the normally irrepressible Gehry has produced. Childs's announced collaboration with Gehry and Venturi, Rauch and Scott Brown for the Massachusetts Museum of Contemporary Art in North Adams, Massachusetts speaks of the uneasiness even cultural clients often have in dealing with the avant-garde as opposed to the big firms. And in a reverse twist, innovative architects working in joint ventures with big firms are desired by clients primarily as designer labels to confer cachet at a time when architects are being increasingly recognized as artists.

Given the difficulties of architectural practice for even the most critically acclaimed professionals, there is no doubt that the big firms will always be able to attract their share of willing young talent, some of whom will find a secure and agreeable niche in organizations where they are spared the pressures of getting work even while paying the price of repetitive activity within the typical extreme division of labor. Other personality types will be attracted to the big firms because of the glittering promise of large-scale work, public visibility, and high pay. Those with a sense of history will be mindful of how even as great a genius as Louis Sullivan could fall from eminence as the head of a big firm because of the effect that conservative trends in social values can have on large-scale public architecture. After Sullivan's career as the greatest architect of tall buildings collapsed, only a new clientele rooted in the progressive movement in the rural Midwest responded to his particular brand of American individuality, resulting in his memorable, late sequence of small banks in small towns.

The generation of American architects who were educated during the late sixties and early seventies are now entering the first truly productive portions of their careers as they enter their forties. Many of them seem much less taken with the traditional notion that greatness in size equates with greatness in achievement. In a recent interview, Steven Holl gave voice to reservations that seem well-founded on the evidence of the work built by the big firms since 1976. "One looks at the big, speculative office building over the past ten years and one sees a paltry, paltry building type indeed: too big, always with a nervous, kinky skin decorating the outside . . . The irony is that these gigantic programs are belied even by the architects who have the commissions. They say, 'Yes, it's too tall, but we're trying to make it acceptable.' Well, I think that's specious reasoning . . . If you look at American architecture as a whole, it's very hard to make the case that the tall building is the receptacle of our greatest aspirations." The same must be said for the overwhelming portion of the work emanating from the big American firms since 1976, landmarks of uncertain direction during an equally uncertain time in our life as a nation.

TOWARD A POST-ANALYTIC ARCHITECTURE
RECENT WORK OF VENTURI, RAUCH AND SCOTT BROWN

ALAN J. PLATTUS

IT IS NOT THE LEAST VIRTUE of the recent work of Venturi, Rauch and Scott Brown (VRSB) that it helps us appreciate more fully their early work and writings. That is not to deny the powerful impact of those extraordinary and disturbing apparitions of the 1960s, but rather to suggest that perhaps the very shock of their challenge, and subsequent efforts to assimilate, to ward off, or "to learn" too literally and quickly from that challenge, obscured their deeper and continuing significance. We have now seen, on the one hand, the extended development of the ostensible plaintiff's brief on behalf of "modernism," and in some cases the actual return of the repressed, and, on the other hand, the various directions taken by presumptive followers who seem to have lost, or in fact never caught, the original scent. More importantly, we have seen—and can go see—an ongoing series of major public projects by VRSB that, in the midst of "other developments," continue to confront one with the central themes of their work, now writ large for those of us who had trouble with the small print of first editions.

One cannot endow these latest works with the shock value of the early projects and texts, and many would no doubt say, correctly in their terms, that the latest works confirm the worst suspicions about what Venturi was up to all along. However I wish to argue, with at least enough rhetorical force to provoke the discussion that these projects deserve, that what Venturi was up to all along anticipates, participates in, and quite possibly pulls the rug out from under a great deal of what passes for current critical debate in architecture. The outlines of that argument go as follows.

First of all, American architecture has always been—with certain exceptions that prove the rule—fundamentally modern in the most interesting, important, and straightforward sense: namely, programmatically and technologically modern. Secondly, there has been a significant, if largely unrecognized, radical, and (dare I say) "deconstructive" strain in American culture in general and architecture in particular since the nineteenth century. Finally, the work of VRSB exemplifies both of those aspects of American architecture, recognizes their oblique relationship to each other, and raises them to a level of self-consciousness and rhetorical expression that makes them central to the work of the firm.

There are at least two largely negative corollaries to these non-axiomatic premises with which I begin. The first is that the work of VRSB is not best seen as the first, or founding, moment of what has been called postmodernism. Certainly their work has been interpreted as such to the point where it may seem to be, ironically, the case. I would, however, argue for locating their work and writings among the most interesting and mature examples of American modernism, and, in any case, as some of the most profound interpretations of the European modernist tradition in relation to American culture. This point has been made quite often, but has not, apparently, sunk in.

The second corollary—more argumentative, and perhaps largely irrelevant—is that the work of VRSB may in fact be, in pursuit of its own agenda, the recent American architecture that best lends itself to an account in terms of deconstruction. I will, however, partially evade the issue by suggesting a different name and set of affiliations as a qualification of that peculiar and problematic designation.

The modernity of American architecture, and even more importantly, American urbanism, is a function of the peculiar mix of extreme self-consciousness and apparent naivete that might be said to characterize American culture in general. In fact it is tempting to argue that American culture passes from modernity to postmodernism, bypassing "modernism" altogether, at the point at which it allows others to define and circumscribe the "true meaning" of modernity. In any case, when Sears Roebuck, in their catalogues of the early twentieth century, proudly announced the general availability of "Modern Homes" for the masses, it seemed clear that they had in mind many of the same things that Le Corbusier wanted to embody in his Citrohan House projects of the twenties, but with a blissful, and perhaps thoroughly modern, lack of anxiety about the stylistic expression or rhetorical embellishment of modern life, modern technique, and modern production and consumption.

There are, of course, a large number of people who could never be content with the mere substance of modernity, but needed its genuine appearance as well. The Westinghouse "Home of Tomorrow," built in 1934 in the heart of the country (Mansfield, Ohio), was already seen as something comically (or tragically) atavistic, the more so since its hopelessly conventional forms "masked" the latest in modern equipment associated with the functions of a more or less conventional domesticity. European visitors were, and apparently still are, fond of simultaneously "discovering"and singing the praises of such unselfconscious modernity, while poking fun at its inconsistencies and contradictions. Lurking behind this persistent need to make external appearance literally and conceptually transparent to the functional and technological guts and bones is a disappointingly simplistic critical model.

It is not without interest that the critical model within which this prescriptive definition of modernism has been inscribed, and in which it often seems to be trapped, was first specifically deployed in a decidedly anti-modern context. Augustus Pugin's Contrasts of 1837 is, in terms of its tone and critical strategy, if not its ideology, seminal for the development of modern architectural polemics. The thoroughly dualistic model of us vs. them, black vs. white, ancient vs. modern, truth vs. the world, has been reactivated time and again, often by means of the merest reversal of terms. Le Corbusier uses it, brilliantly and with literally devastating effect, against the Beaux-Arts; Leon Krier turns it around and uses it against Le Corbusier; and Robert Venturi and Denise Scott Brown have themselves been no mean practitioners of the technique in question. However, their version of Pugin's polarities, in which, for example, their Guild House of 1963 is compared to Paul Rudolph's Crawford Manor of 1965, should not be understood as another rehearsal (and reversal) of the same old opposition. The buildings in question, especially in the light of what has come since, contrast a sort of vernacular modernism against a heroic or even transcendental modernism, where the architect, the building, and even the city walk away from the very problems they presume to solve. That distinction, and its affiliation with the pragmatic version of American modernism, was perhaps not so easy to see in the mid-sixties.

We have, I think, been too distracted by one of the most brilliant and disturbing uses of the aforementioned critical model, namely Venturi and Scott Brown's formulation of the duck vs. decorated shed phenomenon. On the one hand, that piece of polemical artistry is an amazingly prescient diagnosis of the architectural symptoms of a general cultural problem. We have since learned to describe this problem in terms of the radical disjunction of signifier and signified. On the other hand, that pervasive condition was too quickly read as a split between two kinds, or schools, of architecture. One accepted—or acquiesced in—that condition, and the other attempted to heal the rupture. It seems far more interesting to entertain the possibility that the apparent dualism was itself relative and contingent, and that ducks and decorated sheds exist on some sort of a continuum, and are part of the same discursive formation.

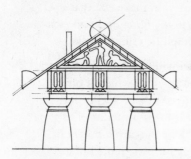

If one looks, for example, at the Tuscan cottage that is part of VRSB's "Eclectic House Series" of 1978, one can identify an ingenious and even further condensed version of nothing other than the Corbusian Citrohan House (especially the 1922 version), in which the double cube of the original has been simultaneously boiled down to a single cube, and dressed up as the little temple it always was. The whole process is not unlike what actually happened to some of Citrohan's offspring at Pessac, which were subjected to the vicissitudes of habitation and vernacular transformations.

The eye and, more importantly, the judgmental faculty tend to be arrested by the Tuscan porch rather than by the persistent and persistently problematic signifier of the "modern dwelling unit." Again, we have been inevitably, and perhaps willingly, distracted by the rhetorical imagery floating across the surface of VRSB's recent buildings. We are, of course, meant to be distracted, but eventually put on, not off, the scent. These apparently promiscuous rhetorical figures, like the heraldic frontispiece above the entrance to Wu Hall at Princeton, are, as Steven Kieran has pointed out, much like a piece of early Renaissance rhetoric attached to a fundamentally medieval building. The question is not which Serlio chimneypiece serves as the model, or which version of a traditional bay window on the Princeton campus inspires the nose cones of Wu Hall, but rather to what extent are the figures seen, and shown, to float across the surface of a building that, upon closer examination, can be understood as typologically and anatomically modern?

The best test of this proposition is to follow the transformation of various traditional spatial and figurative themes in relation to the characteristically modern conditions to which those themes are ultimately seen to be subordinate. For example, to return again to Wu Hall, the dining hall is taken as an exercise in alluding to, without fully realizing, the familiar collegiate type of the "old Gothic hall." This new "old Gothic hall" is subjected to the constraints

Wu Hall, 1983

imposed by the "frozen section" of modern architecture while its perimeter shows evidence of a flirtation with the "free plan." The constriction of a horizontal sandwich of space is thus accepted as a more or less normative condition by VRSB in this and other projects, but is given greater dialectical energy by its confrontation with an illicit desire for a positive spatial figure. The inevitable dominance of a recognizably modern condition is finally confirmed, appropriately enough, at the level of details. These details are frankly modern—or rather, contemporary—as is the treatment of the program (and the equipment that serves it), which makes an issue of the confrontation of the cafeteria and the great hall.

The same argument is rehearsed again by the more notorious facades, where the taut, thin plane demonstrates not only its compositional freedom relative to the programmatic and constructional substance of the building, but also its ability to sustain and ultimately absorb seemingly endless qualification of its primary mission. While ambitious public buildings like Wu Hall may be allowed to indulge in various conceptual figure-ground reversals between, for instance, the horizontal continuity of ribbon windows and the provisional focus of an atavistic round arch, more "ordinary" modern buildings are allowed to remain, for the most part, just that. If one looks at what might be called the meat and potatoes of a contemporary practice—something that VRSB has not eschewed at all, but taken into the realm of its ongoing investigations—one sees the extent to which an office building on the streets of Philadelphia (Institute of Scientific Information) or an unbuilt project for the streets of Baghdad (Khulafa Street Building) mainly decorate and slightly embellish a ubiquitous modern type.

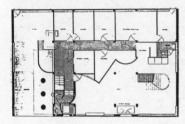

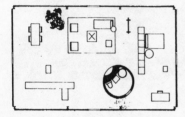

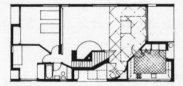

None of this is especially new, either in the firm's work or in the criticism of it. But looking back now it is clear that much of the impetus for future development was actually stored in the ongoing elaboration of themes and issues already on the agenda, rather than in what seemed to be the first steps on the road—a road ultimately not taken by VRSB—to revivalism. We have, for example, already alluded to Le Corbusier's formulation of the problem of the modern house. In his famous diagram of the four house types, Le Corbusier identifies the most difficult—but also most spiritually satisfying—version of this problem as that of packing the characteristically difficult, asymmetrical, episodic, and complex modern domestic program into a very simple and pure constraining volume. That would seem to be precisely the task taken on by Robert Venturi in his mother's house in Chestnut Hill of 1962, but with an even greater degree of difficulty; Venturi attempts to pack in fragmentary allusions to traditional domestic forms and spaces along with all that functional energy. For both Venturi and Le Corbusier, the agenda is set by that pervasively modern condition of programmatic specificity in relation to the constraints, as well as the opportunities, of modern construction. The real antagonist is reductivism or, more precisely, a reductivist attitude toward the ingredients of a potentially modern dialectic. This might be represented by a plan like that of Philip Johnson's Glass House, where all the stuffing has been knocked out of the simple volumetric container in the interest of an image of domesticity closer to the "Primitive Hut" than to the heterotopian modernity of Corbusier and Venturi.

This notion of a spatial discourse that opens, rather than closes, questions is echoed in the urbanistic and site-planning strategies employed by VRSB, especially in its more recent work. Once again, Wu Hall seems to be chrono-logically and conceptually pivotal. It is a building that does not simply fill a site, like wet concrete in a form or a tooth in a gap (as in simplistic versions of contextualism), but rather it actively interrogates a site or, more strongly, invents a site where no clear site seemed to exist. Insofar as it is mainly a single-loaded slab, or a blunt projectile shot into a site and still partially protruding, Wu Hall in its context has unmistakable affinities with the most sophisticated modernist site plans, such as Le Corbusier's Salvation Army Refuge or his plan for St. Dié. Its adjustments are, however, more subtle, and the metaphor suggested is not one of ballistics as much as one of reading be-tween the lines of an existing, and already elliptical, text.

Wu Hall really belongs to none of the recognizable quadrangles that consti-tute the fabric not only of the Princeton campus, but also many American campuses of similar vintage. Rather the building slides out of any definitive context and thereby poses not the "solution" to, but the sign of, a site plan-ning problem of a disparate group of buildings composed—or rather, gerry-mandered—*ex post facto* into a residential college. The components of the newly created Butler College—of which Wu Hall is the social and ad-ministrative "center"—are the buildings of the so-called New Quad and a few older buildings on the other side of a major cross-campus walkway. Wu Hall slips ever so slightly out of one of these groups, gestures toward the other, and begins to negotiate an arrangement between them—not one of unification or resolution, but rather one of an open-ended dialogue. Here, as elsewhere, the relationship to conventional typologies (in this case the col-legiate quadrangle) is one of simultaneous engagement and difference. The result, while it may be clearly related to the firm's stated theoretical positions, is neither predictable nor circumscribed by those positions. It is both more subtle and, in its extraordinary economy of means in relation to the heterogeneity of both program and site, far more direct.

It is, then, no surprise to find that Wu Hall is not only a turning point in VRSB's institutional work, it is also a starting point for an extended series of ongoing cognate investigations. These investigations have included other campus buildings, both classrooms and laboratories, and several museums. The diverse elements of these programs are initially submitted to the dis-cipline of a fairly straightforward prismatic container, tending toward a simple single- or double-loaded extrusion, but are then pushed and pulled and prodded in relation to both programmatic and contextual pressures. The approach is perhaps best understood in relation to Louis Kahn's "form and design" method, in which the program is conceptualized in terms of an ideal spatial figure that becomes the repetitive module of the whole scheme. One moves from the "order of the room" to the "order of the institution" and

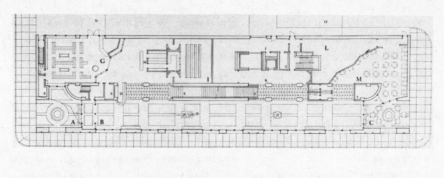

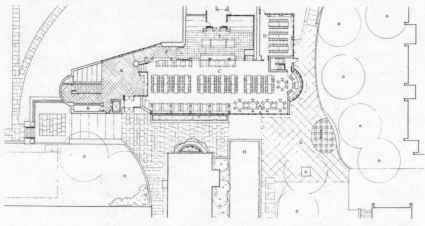

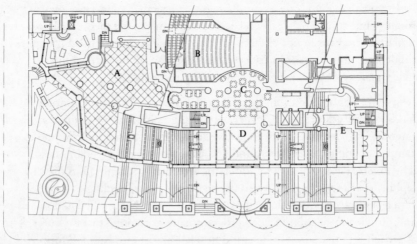

(Top to bottom)
Laguna Gloria Art Museum, 1985, ground floor plan
Wu Hall, 1983, first floor plan
Seattle Art Museum, 1987, composite plan

presumably on to the order of the city, "order" being understood to be per-vasive and, hopefully, definitive. For Kahn, the ideal spatial unit also provided the structural order of the building.

In contrast to this persistent search for order and authority, a series of projects by VRSB—from Wu Hall to the Laguna Gloria Museum in Austin, Texas, to the Seattle Art Museum, and beyond—dramatizes the incommensurability of the competing demands of program, type, structure, context, and image, hovers on the brink of architectonic entropy, but always returns to a remark-ably concise overall form. In particular, the free plan is both a rhetorical ges-ture and an accommodation of the often exaggerated complexities of the program within a modern structure. The Seattle project exemplifies these conditions while developing the lateral confrontation with a street that in Wu Hall holds out the promise of an arcade without being able to make room for it. The Seattle Art Museum's street extends that layered condition into the depth of the site where it meets up with a compacted, incipient ex-plosion of spaces within. The energy inside and out is emphasized by the ap-parently casual but very precise and willful nipping off corners.

In these respects, the Seattle project looks both back and forward: back in a particularly poignant way to the unbuilt project for the Yale Mathematics Building, surely one of the most precocious compositions of the six-ties; forward to what promises to become one of the most provocative of VRSB's recent projects, namely the Sainsbury Wing addition to the National Gallery in London. The National Gallery project extends the ex-ploration of the confrontation of the free plan with the irregular and circumstantially distorted perimeter, here made all the more remarkable by the adjacency of an apparently traditional set of galleries on the upper floor. That is the truly radical implication of the free plan: not merely its ability to accommodate dif-ferent spatial arrangements on different floors, but its ability to produce dif-ferent spatial worlds in immediate juxtaposition. Many architects and critics have remarked on the characteristically modern, but also peculiarly American, qualities of this sort of juxtaposition, not only in such extreme cases as Disneyland, but also in "ordinary" towns, landscapes, and buildings. Most have quickly registered their disapproval, and even those who adopt a more celebratory tone seem to absorb and aestheticize the heterogeneity. It will, then, be interesting to see what is made of the re-presentation of that provincial heterogeneity in the heart of imperial London.

The Sainsbury Wing seems already to have posed a challenge for the conventional tools of critical and academic consumption, namely those of "architectural analysis." A recent issue of *Architectural Design*[1] featured an article by Geoffrey Baker entitled "A Formal Analysis of Stirling's Unsuccessful Proposal for the National Gallery Extension, London." Baker's essay is an apparently rigorous and closely reasoned defense of James Stirling and Michael Wilford's entry in the limited competition of 1986, from which the VRSB scheme emerged victorious. If you accept the terms—and the limits—of Baker's argument, you will be led, logically, to admit that Stirling's "unsuccessful proposal" was in fact a, if not the, "successful solution" to the problem posed by the program and the site. By implication, and Baker studiously avoids a direct comparison, the VRSB scheme does not hold up to such a rigorously analytical interrogation. Indeed, I think anyone would agree that something else is going on in VRSB's project—something largely incomprehensible, and certainly indigestible, from a strictly analytic point of view.

Mark Linder has taken this line of discussion much further in his Yale M.E.D. thesis of 1988, wherein he proposes a parallel between the approach exemplified by the VRSB National Gallery project and some recent developments in American philosophy, particularly in the neo-pragmatist criticism of Richard Rorty. In that work—which invokes the critique of philosophy proposed by Derrida and other post-structuralists—the orthodox analytic

National Galery Extension, 1986

tradition of Anglo-American philosophy is subjected to a critique not unlike the critique of architectural orthodoxy, modernist and otherwise, developed by Venturi. "Post-analytic," the label used in a recent anthology of philosophical essays in this vein edited by John Rajchman and Cornel West, seems remarkably apt to describe what VRSB is up to in many recent projects. Furthermore, the portrait of the philosopher as a "liberal ironist," painted by Rorty in his recent book, *Contingency, Irony and Solidarity*, might be that of Robert Venturi and Denise Scott Brown in any number of respects. The parallel model of philosophy as a sort of ongoing and even inconclusive conversation, rather than a rigorous analytic exercise or a definitive ontological grounding of things beyond time and place, is an attractive characterization of relationships developed in a project like the Sainsbury Wing, with its difficult context and circumstances.

That is not to say that VRSB has not been, on notable occasions, guilty of what I suppose we should now call the "analytic fallacy" of building, too directly and literally, an analytic diagram or theoretical proposition. Of course the heuristic value of a project like that for the National Football Hall of Fame of 1967 is exceeded only by the pure pleasure it would have been had it been built. More worrisome is the tendency, in *Learning From Las Vegas* and certain projects deriving from it, to subject the radical heterogeneity of the vernacular landscape to a reductive analysis that begins to look rather academic in its format if not in its intentions. Nothing could be further from the *tour de force* proposed for the Sainsbury Wing that, for all its thoughtful consideration of the program and the site, is neither predicated upon or predicted by any single model or method in the architectural arsenal unless it be that distinctly nontheoretical model of a conversation. The voice assumed by the new wing is uniquely its own—voluble and insistent as it breaks in on the measured cadences of the Wilkins facade with a jumbled outburst of columns; distant, quiet, and almost mute in the single, partially disengaged column that culminates the discourse—but incomprehensible as a monologue in isolation from its interlocutors. In this respect, as well as in its unpredictable eruption, it reminds us of an earlier conversation between columns.

I refer, of course, to the notorious ironic/iconic/ionic column that marks the gap, and measures the distance, between old and new in the 1973 VRSB addition to the Allen Art Museum at Oberlin College. That column, seen in context, as it so rarely is, clearly participates in a rather extraordinary discussion involving the frankly pragmatic modern columns (cylindrical concrete and exposed steel) of the addition and the applied pilasters of the original Cass Gilbert museum. Ultimately, that discussion is about the problem of adding to a gracefully self-assured institutional monument to high culture, a building that fronts the principal space of the town as well as the campus. The original

Allen Memorial Art Museum, 1973
Two views of ironic/iconic/ionic column

museum announces and explains itself quite clearly, and even seems to contain the rules for its own expansion. Indeed, those rules were followed by an
addition in the 1930s that extends the original courtyard building along its
major axis by means of another courtyard. However VRSB conspicuously
and self-consciously avoids both the predictable and analytically correct ways
of attaching to the host building and the other equally predictable extreme of
total disjunction. The attachment along an edge rather than in relation to an
axial center and the development of their addition in three dimensions high-
light both the local contingency of the compositional process and the general
cultural contingency of the representational mechanism invoked by the
museum as architecture and as institution. If the sign of the cultural con-
fidence and authority of the original building and its first addition is found in
the lovely Renaissance fountain at the corner of the building, then the signs
of the current condition are the Oldenburg plug, which mimics the abrupt attachment visible from the front of the ensemble, and the infamous column,
which articulates the lack of any positive attachment at the rear of the building. Finally, that column appears again as an object in the museum's collection, as seen from within the gallery through the window that replaces a summarily chamfered corner.

Already, in 1978, Alan Colquhoun had pointed out the radical consequences
suggested by Oberlin's development of the argument sketched out in *Learning From Las Vegas*. But because Colquhoun saw the discontinuity articulated
by VRSB—between old and new, but also between signifier and signified—

as a largely pessimistic commentary on a condition from which there is, according to the terms of the argument, no escape, he draws mainly negative conclusions about its prospects. Certainly, it could not be the basis for a positive "theory of architecture." However, it might be, along the lines already suggested, the opening of a discussion—with and about tradition, among other things—albeit one in which separate discourses will never be wholly commensurable or translatable, one into the other, and problems will never be "resolved." And yet the conversation overheard from the old portico of the National Gallery, with one ear cocked toward the monumental assertions of Nelson's Column in the center of Trafalgar Square and the other attuned to the discordant harmony sung by the lone detached column of the Sainsbury Wing, is worth attention. If it seems somewhat desultory, and at the same time thoroughly reflexive, might it not be a disarmingly accurate microcosm of a pervasive cultural and discursive condition?

It is somewhere in the vicinity of this condition that post-analytic dialogue overlaps with post-structuralist deconstruction. Although I am inclined to be very tentative about such a proposal, there is value in provocation to suggest that VRSB may have anticipated much of the current agenda with respect to a critique of representation, radical textuality, and the free play of signifiers. I would, in any case, argue that post-structuralist criticism is fundamentally anti-reductive. To initiate a critical architecture by first reducing the text (and the context) to a network of abstract points, lines, and planes, or vectors of force, seems suspicious; VRSB, at least, plays the game with a full deck, and engages the texts in question in all their linguistic heterogeneity and instability.

In this respect, and in many other important ones, they have a great deal more in common with Frank Gehry than, for example, with Peter Eisenman. In projects like his own house in Santa Monica and the recent renovation of a Back Bay office building in Boston (more than in those projects that seem to represent typological collisions) Gehry develops his own unique version of an incremental and opportunistic attitude toward the transformation of existing conditions. As in the work of VRSB, these transformations far exceed the limited expectations of an analytic account of the objects in question, becoming almost "monstrous" in their critical distortion of a normative discourse, which they nevertheless acknowledge. Some would suggest that this is what American architecture and urbanism have done all along with respect to the normative models and canons of the European tradition. George Hersey has characterized that condition as "American bastardy," and, if we accept such a diagnosis, then VRSB and Gehry are, in their interventions and additions, re-producing second generation illegitimacy fathered upon the already suspect offspring of more noble parentage. In any case, they seem to accept, and even celebrate, the impure problem of addition as the paradigm of architectural activity in contemporary America.

The various strategies used by architects to formulate and address the problem of addition constitute a topic worthy of extensive study. If we take the case already seen to be the most visible, and perhaps even emblematic, occasion for raising the problem in its full cultural dimension, namely that of museum additions, we can see that VRSB's work lies somewhere between the seamless continuity of John Barrington Bayley's addition to the Frick Museum and the virtual absorption of one discourse by a totally different sort, as in Michael Graves's original project for the Whitney Museum. We may consider both those strategies to be "problematic," but neither actually "problematizes" the condition itself in a way that keeps open (rather than attempts a definitive closure of) the question on the table. The crucial difference is, of course, the belief manifest by the Frick addition in the possibility—indeed, the necessity—of cultural as well as architectural continuity; or, in the case of Graves, a belief in an alternative set of values. This contrasts VRSB's reluctance to endorse any single, presumptively authoritative position vis-à-vis the given circumstances.

Graves and Venturi have, of course, crossed paths at significant points, as a comparison between the Chestnut Hill House of 1962 and Graves' Plocek House in Warren, New Jersey will readily show. But they were, I think, headed in dramatically different directions. As Peggy Deamer has suggested, Graves' work has been consistently committed, in both early and late transformations, to the search for a set of fundamental principles, grounded in a phenomenological account of the position of the subject in relation to the elements and forms of architecture and the larger landscape. This sort of grounded, even essentialist, discourse has always been the subject of extreme skepticism in the writing and projects of VRSB. In his Gropius lecture of 1982 at Harvard, Robert Venturi called attention to the depth of this distinction between himself and Graves, as well as the general direction taken by a "postmodernism" that often took him, almost for granted, as founding father figure. Whether or not VRSB can now be embraced in the rather broader account of postmodernism (associated with the position of someone like Jean Francois Lyotard), it remains clear that vis-à-vis the directions taken by Graves and others, VRSB's position is decidedly, and significantly, post-romantic. It invokes tradition as a body of contingent and even arbitrary conventions, not as a body of deeply rooted myth—or, if those myths are explored, they are looked at with critical detachment, not reinvested with cultural authority.

Similar points can, and have, been made with respect to the comparison of divergent directions taken by VRSB and architects like Alan Greenberg or

Robert Stern, who started from similar points of departure. VRSB's version of Mt. Vernon for the Brants exaggerates the vernacular idiosyncracies of the original while condensing the field in which they are deployed; it was eventually rejected in favor of Greenberg's "corrected" version, which lets the air out of the original by relaxing and expanding the field. The same distinction is already latent in two superficially more similar projects by VRSB and Stern from the early seventies. VRSB's first house for the Brants in Greenwich, Connecticut and a slightly later house by Stern in Westchester County, New York exploit the juxtapositions and adjacencies of a more or less free plan, deploying a heterogeneous vocabulary in an episodic manner, all within a tightly packed, even bulging, container. But, already, the condensation and economy of gesture of the VRSB project is in contrast to the much more literal and (dare I say) extravagant project by Stern. This difference is exaggerated further along the time line. Venturi's first project for the Millard Meiss House of 1962 uses many of the same domestic elements and images as a recent house by Stern in Farm Neck, Massachusetts. While Stern develops the expansive continuities of the shingle style as a way of accommodating a multiplicity of elements, gestures, and programmatic ingredients, Venturi condenses and exaggerates the unresolved confrontation of different volumes and even types.

The real basis of this contrast lies, I think, at a level deeper than mere compositional preference and raises one of the two points I would like to reiterate in summarizing the achievement of VRSB. The principal models upon which Stern draws are, from the outset, found mainly in the realm of name brand architecture or, as a student of mine once put it, house styles of the rich and famous. VRSB combine a profound knowledge and respect for these models with a fundamental, and generally overriding, appreciation of the vernacular, with its conceptual and literal economy of form and expression. For so many modern architects, from Voysey, McIntosh, and Olbrich to Le Corbusier, Rossi, and Gehry (but not for Stern or, for that matter, Eisenman), the vernacular provides a source of energy and a model of restraint. (Through projects such as the Trubeck and Wislocki Houses of 1972, this direction has inspired a significant number of younger American architects now working away temporarily—one hopes—in the shadow of the neo-avant-garde.) In the work of VRSB, this approach carries over into the public realm as well. If one compares their early project for a Town Center in North Canton, Ohio with a project of equally conspicuous centrality to the life of a small American community, Graves's Fargo-Morehead Cultural Bridge of 1978, a familiar contrast emerges. Graves's extraordinary bridge is confidently monumental and confirms its position in the world by alluding to a set of cosmic relationships embedded in the landscape and reflected in anthropomorphic imagery. The project treats those relationships, or at least encourages us to think of them, as timeless and universal. The values invoked by the North Canton project seem, on the other hand, local, even homely, and thoroughly conventional. The forms may echo the civic centers of Aalto, lifted artificially above the flat expanse of the Finnish landscape, or even the hill towns of Italy, emboldening me to borrow the term "civic humanism" from the great historian Hans Baron to characterize the aspirations of these projects.

However, that humanism must remain provisional and contingent, since the architects recognize that it is no longer rooted in either an unchanging landscape or a deeply rooted set of shared values. We are no longer members of any conceivable organic community, but can still share, in our plight, what Rorty calls a sense of solidarity. Thus the particular circumstances in which we find ourselves are cast, not as an inescapable impasse, but as a rather tight spot, from which we must extricate ourselves not by blasting our way free, but by means of a continuous and open conversation.

1. Architectural Design, vol. 57, no. 1/2 (1987).

FROM STRUCTURE TO SITE TO TEXT:
EISENMAN'S TRAJECTORY

K. MICHAEL HAYS

THE PROJECT FOR THE CANNAREGIO DISTRICT in Venice, 1978, is a pivotal point in the architectural research of Peter Eisenman. It focuses several theoretical issues that will be the threads of my thesis: (1) the assimilation and elaboration of certain structuralist tenets in the architecture of the last twelve years; (2) the protraction of certain modernist modes of perception that involve the critical negation of the object as a unique, purely visual, or aesthetic form;[1] and (3) the movement in Eisenman's work, propelled by his assimilation of modernism and structuralism, from structure to site to text. Here we will want to gauge, however tentatively, Eisenman's movement as either a progression or a regression in terms of its relationship to larger cultural and disciplinary frameworks.

Eisenman's work prior to Cannaregio was concerned almost exclusively with isolating and elaborating those architectural elements and operations that would both ensure a specific autonomy and self-referentiality of the architectural object, and verify and purify the object in resistance to certain encircling determinants. One such determinant is physical construction and materiality: Eisenman's notion of "cardboard" architecture unloads the physical object of all traditional senses of building. A second determinant is its actual use: his notion of "postfunctionalism" shifts our engagement with form from utilization to consideration of architectural ele-

ments as signals or notations for a conceptual state of the object. A third
determinant is all contextual, narrative, or associational potentials: his emphasis on the syntactic over the semantic dimension of form proposes on behalf of an architect a *competence* or knowledge of his discipline, understood as
an internalized system of architectural principles and underlying rules of combination. It stresses the deep, conceptual structures from which various architectures can be generated over the surface, perceptual characteristics of
any particular architectural instance. Eisenman's early work thus incorporates
two standard structuralist principles: the bracketing off of the context, both
physical and historical, and, with that, the bracketing off of the individual
subject in favor of a notion of an intersubjective architectural system of signification that, like language, pre-dates any individual and is much less his or
her product than he or she is the product of it.

Eisenman's turn to structuralism in his early work is part of a more general attempt to theorize architecture in the 1970s. Structuralist criticisms, and the
corollary developments in linguistics, structural anthropology, and literary
criticism, offered analogous frameworks and strategies for thinking architecture back into its own as a discipline, a practice, and a mode of knowledge
with a specific tradition and structure. And this disciplinary discourse came to
be seen, in some form, as *the* condition of meaning in architecture—whether
conceived as an enabling condition for architecture's continued intelligibility
that should be elaborated, or as a coercive constraint of a hegemonic institution that should be dismantled.[2]

If there were the seeds here of an architecture at once self-conscious of its
own disciplinary conventions, and mindful of a social theory of meaning,
they were not, on the whole, developed by the architects most often compared to Eisenman during this formative period. The necessarily practical
aspects of architecture led many architects toward various attempts to re-
ground the disciplinary conventions and procedures uncovered and analyzed
by structuralism. Perhaps this was necessary and inevitable. Yet in such re-
grounding, structuralism's critical edge was lost.

And so, for example, in Richard Meier's work, which elaborates compositional techniques seemingly similar to those of Eisenman, syntactical and
typological inventions become the basis for reconnecting the architectural
sign with its functional vocation and disciplinary conventions. Meier assimi-
lates the critical, analytical, and often negational tendencies of modernism
and its structuralist interpreters, reconnects the architectural sign to the
referential realm that structuralism had evacuated, and demonstrates the
availability of seemingly autonomous or critical formal manipulations for institutionalized and domesticated ends. Previously worked-out aesthetic structures reappear in his work as historical simulacra without any cultural reflec-

tion, serving merely to prop up the myth of cultural continuity and progress, as if their chic monumentality and awe-inspiring physical presence compensated for a seemingly unchangeable social status quo.

On the other hand, John Hejduk regrounds his work in terms of the individual body. While his work disavows the classical humanist view of Michael Graves—that is, of the unified human body as both a point of departure and a final, idealized representation—Hejduk nevertheless renovates the body and the phenomenology of its representation as orientation points that might prove resistant to uncritical, merely formal games.

In a society such as ours where objects appear alienated and cut off from human purpose, this return to the body can become a consoling doctrine: the world is grasped in relation to *me*, as a correlate of *my* body and *my* consciousness. And this is reassuring; it restores the individual subject—which modernism challenged and structuralism proper sought to liquidate—to its rightful throne, seen as the source and origin of all meaning. In this sense, Hejduk's "poetic" architecture recovers and refurbishes the old dream of the bourgeoisie, whose ideology had hinged on the belief that the individual subject was somehow prior to and in control of its own history and social conditions.

We can theorize this using a simplified version of Jacque Lacan's metaphor of the mirror image of the subject. Lacan's so-called "mirror stage" of development serves as an exemplary situation of how the subject is structured with respect to the body.[3] The mirror stage denotes that moment when the child acquires a sense of its own bodily unity through a process of identification with an external object, the image in the mirror. The apprehension of bodily unity is the support of the division between a coherent self and that "other" against which the self is perceived. For the very exteriority of the mirror image anticipates what will become in Lacan's account the fundamental characteristic of the ego: a narcissistic mirage of coherence and centrality through which the subject is seduced into misrecognizing its actual alienation and fragmentation. In the mirror the child finds reflected back to itself a gratifyingly unified and responsive image of itself (the child moves its arm, the mirror obliges in kind.) The identification with an image of one's self is constitutive of that self, and this constitution is the structural precondition for any ideological manipulation or massage of the subject.

Architecture based on the human body similarly lures the ego by offering an image of its mirror-self. This is a condition that Hejduk's work at once exemplifies and questions. In many of Hejduk's objects, the viewer encounters an architecture overtly anthropomorphic but not quite human. We see not so much a reflection of ourselves as a shadow or a distortion—an image that dis-

turbs the narcissistic gaze of the viewer through what might be called an "in-
mixing of otherness," presenting itself as *other* to our body and our subjectivity. The differential play between subject and object that takes place along
the axis of viewer and representation in the mirror metaphor now finds its
analogue *in the object itself*. The subject having been split from its object by
the logic of social and symbolic reification, the object must now be
reconstructed by Hejduk in such a way as to bear the place of the subject
within itself. Like the animals in a fable who speak with human voices,
Hejduk's objects are the obverse of classical humanist representations. They
do not render to us our narcissistic object of desire so directly, but they nonetheless restore the individual subjectivity (which structuralism had displaced)
in objects that can be seen as parables of a privileged because private
psychological moment.[3]

Whatever the strengths of these positions of Meier, Graves, and Hejduk, all
attempt to restore the symbolic authenticity of content and authorship in an
era when such notions have become increasingly problematic. All attempt to
re-bound architecture, to re-colonize it within received conceptions of cultural institutions, functionality, individuality, and contemplative reception.

Elaborating Lacan's analysis can lead us to theorize another sort of design
practice. We recognize with Lacan that the self-creating and self-representing
ego is a function or effect of a subject that in actuality is always dispersed,
never identical with itself, strung out along the chains of the discourses that
constitute it. There is a radical gap between the subject, split into several in-
commensurable faculties by the various institutions that place contradictory
ideological demands on it, and the representation of that subject through the
work of art, as in that desired state consisting in a harmony between those
faculties. Certain artistic practices, rather than present conventionalized architectural signs or spaces that are likely to gain our assent more readily, confront us with the very institutional apparatuses that legitimate the processes of
architectural sign production by making the mechanisms of their representation part of their actual content, which is bound to result in a self-con-
tradictory aesthetic. The so-called "alienation-effects" of advanced modernist
art turn this contradiction to fruitful use, positing society, culture, technology, and art's own disciplinary institutions as determinant facts, but at the
same time unmasking them as coercive and incomplete. Among the finest examples of this sort of production are Brechtian theater, certain Russian avant-
garde experiments, Dadaism, and other modernist practices that employ techniques of estrangement or alienation-effects to political ends.

The work of Peter Eisenman situates itself in the line descending from some
of these practices. It begins with two fundamental assumptions of modernist
production: (1) the advancement of artistic forms of a society is linked to the

advancement of its technical means, and (2) transformations of social structures necessitate the transformation of aesthetic hierarchies and require radically new and different forms of perception. Taken together these two assumptions form the basis for the modernist insistence on the absolute contemporaneity of subjects, materials, technologies, and procedures of design, and,
consequently, for the critical negation of the work of art as a unique object.[4]

Eisenman has been explicit about his interest in post-nuclear technologies,
chaos theory, and fractal geometry and in their effects on contemporary culture. Consider the following comment (from an essay on Aldo Rossi):

> *The problem [we face now is] choosing between an anachronistic con-*
> *tinuance of hope and an acceptance of the bare conditions of survival . . .*
> *Incapable of believing in reason, uncertain of the significance of his ob-*
> *jects, man [has lost] his capacity for signifying . . . There is now merely*
> *a landscape of objects; new and old are the same; they appear to have*
> *meaning but they speak into a void of history. The realization of this*
> *void, at once cataclysmic and claustrophobic, demands that past, present,*
> *and future be reconfigured.* To have meaning, both objects and life
> must acknowledge and symbolize this new reality.[5]

What is more, Eisenman follows the modernist paradigm of deploying alienation-effects to reorient our apprehension of architectural form. A publication
by Eisenman in the May, 1974 issue of *Progressive Architecture*, significantly entitled "To Adolf Loos & Bertold Brecht," emphasizes the independent identification of the work, but goes on to state, "In the process of taking posses-
sion [of his own house] the owner begins to destroy, albeit in a positive
sense, the initial unity and completeness of the architectural structure . . . [in-
itiating] a process of inquiry into one's own latent capacity to understand any
man-made space."[6] Now, recognizing that the architectural object in some
sense adequately names that which propels and yet eludes this process of inquiry, we have also broached here a notion of "performativity"—the activity
of *reading* architecture performs and constitutes that which *in the architectural
object alone* can never be complete: namely, the disciplinary-ideological apparatus that legitimates and indeed makes possible the formation of the architectural object in the first place.

In the Cannaregio project, we witness a movement that will henceforth characterize Eisenman's work: the movement from structure to site to text. This
movement is a consequence, I shall argue, of following through on performativity, taking it to its conclusion in a critique of the very fundamental procedures of the discipline that the early works attempt to isolate and codify.

The Cannaregio project is the first Eisenman project in which the site is a
major factor in the signifying practice. The grid of Le Corbusier's unrealized

Project for the Cannaregio District, 1978

Venice Hospital project—itself an emblem of the utopian, salutary ambition of modern architecture and, at the same time, a rationalization of the ad hoc urban structure of Venice—is reduced to a geometrical abstraction and replicated onto the irregular fabric of the adjacent site. Here we have not only an incorporation of the immediate context into the structure of the work, but also an importantly new operation, that of *appropriation* and the concomitant semantic nullification of the image that was confiscated.

Appropriation moves to yet a different dimension in the second operation of Cannaregio. The previously designed House XIa—itself emblematic of the history of its own formation, comprising no more than a series of stills that trace the steps of generation from one state of the object to the next—now becomes the appropriated object. Already depleted of its functional, material, and semantic potentials, the house is devalued even more thoroughly by its repetition across the site and by changes in size from that of a house to a series of objects either smaller than a house or larger than a house, each of which contains nothing but the shell of the next smaller object. And then the topological axis of symmetry of the objects is traced as a cut into the ground, a line that connects the two bridges across the canals that delimit the Cannaregio.[7]

Thus, the boundaries of the site, Eisenman's own earlier work, and Le Corbusier's project are all incorporated into the structure of the new work, now as so many texts that oppose all rooted, symbolic, or solidly signifying usages of dominant and presumedly authentic languages in favor of an architectural material that renounces even the individual architect's aesthetic skill in order to now move toward the discipline's extremities or limits. This is an architecture that is connected not to a pretense of authenticity but to its own abolition— what might be called, with some hesitation, a "deterritorialized" architecture.[8]

In shifting attention toward the extremities of the discipline, Eisenman produces the potential of a direct criticism of architecture's disciplinary presumptions—presumptions about the determinant structure of the site, about architecture's mimetic and representational functions, and about the ideological innocence of form. What I am suggesting here is that Eisenman's strategy is a successor to the de-familiarization and alienation-effects mentioned above, that the layering of the visual texts—the superimposition of two preexisting fabrics (those of Le Corbusier and Venice), the erasure of their use-value, the doubling of this visual text by a second (his own), and the resultant shift of attention to the disciplinary devices that normally frame our understanding of form—operates in a similar way as Barthes's second order sign to shift our attention and reading to the disciplinary-ideological apparatus by which architecture is constituted.

What usually blocks disciplinary self-reflection is the inability to theorize the discipline's own boundaries. Eisenman obliges us to locate the possibility of disciplinary critique, and therefore of critical resistance or fruitful expansion, in the activity of reading the object and attending to the disciplinary conventions and limits that delimit and determine its formation. Again, we return to the notion of performativity. Concretely, this emphasis on performativity implies that the potential of meaningful architectural practice today is produced and made available, at least in part and albeit only in a partial and symbolic mode, in the analyses of the institutional formation of disciplinary objects. Cannaregio dismantles our routine business of designing and looking at form in order to show how those design strategies, which everyone takes for granted as obvious, real, and correct, are actually arbitrary, conventional, and institutional.

Of course, in proposing a kind of politics of *textuality*, a subversion and disruption at the level of the signifier only, Eisenman is also exhibiting a tendency that is relatively common in poststructuralist thought: that of construing a text or object that is disruptive of readers' expectations and conventions as a critically viable gesture in and of itself, purely by virtue of its supposed ability to reveal and counter the assured positions of dominant disciplinary systems. But an interrogation and displacement of the grounds of object formation, of disciplinary procedures, of subjectivity, and so on, often boil down to, *exactly and merely*, interrogations and displacements. We should recognize here that interrogations and displacements of this sort risk becoming a kind of cynicism, that merely pokes a little at the prevailing order without provoking specific actions that might help to dismantle that order. So in construing the Cannaregio project as having a certain critical force, I am insisting that it is by hooking into material institutions—architecture itself as an institution—and not merely by playing with detached forms that Eisenman's work has some ideological teeth.

Henceforth Eisenman's work will elaborate those specific procedures already fully laid out in the Cannaregio project but will split into different trajectories. And in a thorough examination of each of these trajectories, we should be able to evaluate precisely the progress or regression of Eisenman's critique. Here, however, I will be able only to make a few tentative, concluding comments.

The first trajectory I am thinking of comprises the Fin d'Out Hous and the Romeo and Juliette projects. In these projects, Eisenman intends to destabilize, through procedures he designates as "decomposition" and "scaling," the heretofore intransigent centrisms of architecture—presence and origin—that have contributed to the myth of the authenticity of the unique object. In the Romeo and Juliette project the various superimpositions of narrative fictions, city walls, castles, and architectural figures of different scales generate one of the most exuberant exercises in textual production that contemporary architecture has to show—a self-generating sequence of texts whose intersections are multiple and random, for which the original narrative and narrator-architect are mere *pre*texts to the realization of a mechanism for spinning off aleatory and seemingly uncontrollable new configurations out of old anecdotal and formal material. To use a common shorthand, this is architectural textuality fully grown.

But in the reconfiguration of this project in the Architectural Association of London's *Moving Arrows, Eros, and Other Errors* (1986), the once subversive mechanisms of textuality are converted into a reconciliation of the conflict between the media status of the individual designer and the critical negation of the architectural object. The project operates in terms of the inherited modernist dialectic that Benjamin Buchloh has identified as the attempt "to be simultaneously the *exemplary* object of all such commodity production and the *exceptional* object which denied and resisted the universality of that reign."[9] But in comparison with its modernist predecessors like Stéphane Mallarmé's spatialization of linguistic material in *Un coup de dés* or Marcel Broodthaers's elaboration of Mallarmé in *Un coup de dés jamais n'abolira le hasard. Image*, or in comparison to contemporary work in other art practices, *Moving Arrows, Eros, and Other Errors* is more of a delicate compromise, juxtaposing the seemingly anonymous mechanicity of mass reproduction with a highly individualized aesthetic system. The result of this effectively plays into the hands of apparatuses of cultural distribution that find closure in the consumer of art objects. It returns to obsolete notions of cultural production by individual artists in order to give to the media industry the adornment of the radical-chic but critically dysfunctional image that it desires. It reinforces and reaffirms private property and private enterprise without questioning the structuring principle of the commodified sign itself. All this occurs precisely at a historical moment when a reactionary middle class struggles to ensure and expand its privileges, including those of the censorship of intellectual culture and the sanction of artistic activities.

Also following the Cannaregio project, the built works and projected buildings point to a second trajectory. In the Center for the Visual Arts at Ohio State University, for example, the Columbus street grid is projected onto the campus, at once consolidating the stadium, the oval, and the arts center, but also expanding the influence of the building outward in a way similar to Cannaregio. The existing auditoria now become appropriated material. In the Biocenter for the University of Frankfurt the angle of an underground service core already on the site becomes both the organizing line of the scheme and a preexisting datum that disturbs the composition. An altogether different kind of text, that of molecular biology, here transcoded into architectural form interpenetrates with determinants derived from the site. Of course, the choice of the DNA code is anything but arbitrary when seen in our present context: for authors from J. G. Ballard to Jean Baudrillard, the fascination of DNA lies in its status as writing that writes *us* rather than writing that we write. Through this appropriation Eisenman is able to further intensify what has by now become a poststructuralist topos of anxiety about authenticity and subjectivity.

And yet, in these built works, Eisenman confronts a problem that he was able to avoid in the Cannaregio project: the dilemma of the aestheticization of the functional object and the functionalization of the visual sign. Eisenman's response to this dilemma is again precisely modernist—he is reluctant to accept the complete disintegration of the aesthetic object even after Cannaregio's recognition of the radically altered historical circumstances that affect the structural conditions of architectural production and reception. These works try to operate on two levels, as visual signs that negate our unmediated and uncritical perception of the object, and as real functional buildings with cultural use-value dictated by established institutions. Not surprisingly, the contradiction remains unresolved. Yet in their contradictions, they reproduce the structural conditions from which any work of architecture, under the present conditions of total reification, must be constructed: the constant struggle between the two equally intolerable poles of mere obedient service to existing institutions and mere aesthetic voluntarism.

The contradiction of Eisenman's work is that, on the one hand, it participates in the development of hermetic and rarefied procedures through which the architectural sign is constituted and interpreted, and on the other hand, it seems equally determined to investigate the processes of reification that the architectural sign undergoes when it is so constituted and received. This contradiction is a consequence of the insistence, of which I have spoken earlier, on the absolute contemporaneity of subjects, procedures, and perceptions in our present life-world. In Eisenman's own words, "to have meaning, both objects and life must acknowledge and symbolize this new reality [of lost meaning]." And what this condition leads to is a conversion of the anomie of modern society—the social dissolution and fragmentation of present society— into a self-imposed condition of actual, phenomenal fragmentation and dissolution. Eisenman's affiliations here seem to be with those poststructuralists who warn that the aesthetic proposed is not at all a revolutionary one, but a way of surviving under present capitalism, producing new forms of perception and fresh desires within the structural limits of the capitalist mode of production. In Eisenman's work it remains unclear whether all this is an effort that seeks to prepare us for a time when the rubble of distinct and unrelated signifiers—the waste products of capitalism and the seemingly purely negative loss of reality that is engendered—might be imagined as having some positive future sense, or whether this mode of post-signification is just one more demonstration of not only the abolition of architecture as a communicative action or representational practice, not only the evacuation of significations and subjectifications, but also the loss of all dimensions of critique and conscious resistance available to architectural practice.

1. I do not mean here the negation of the actual object, but rather the negation of conceptualization of the object as a purely aesthetic construct. This conceptualization of architecture as pure form stands in contrast to the modernist understanding of the object as a product of systems of reproduction and repetition. See my "Reproduction and Negation: The Cognitive Project of the Avant-Garde," in Beatriz Colomina et al., eds., *Architectureproduction* (New York: Princeton Architectural Press, 1988).

2. It seems quite uncontroversial that the assimilation of certain structuralist tenets into architectural discourse is one of the primary constituents of the period in question. After Colin Rowe's comparative morphological analyses of recurring and reconvertible architectural structures spanning a wide range of scales, times, and cultures—properly structuralist in their bracketing off of the formal procedures from their specific historical determinants and cultural vagaries in favor of a formally rigorous classification and analysis of the very fundamental mechanisms of architecture—or after Robert Venturi's explorations of the intersubjective structures of shared vernaculars and ordinary building—again structuralist in their refusal of a notion of meaning based in individual expression or performance—or after Bernard Tschumi's Manhattan Transcripts, it became increasingly difficult to be satisfied with criticisms based on a purely functional, intentional, or naively historical description of the building.

3. In accusing it of reproducing individualism, I have not been entirely fair to John Hejduk's work. Jeffrey Kipnis and others are currently working on a more generous interpretation of Hejduk's work that will, no doubt, challenge what I have attempted here.

4. I borrow this formulation from Benjamin H. D. Buchloh's essay on Marcel Broodthaers, "Open Letters, Industrial Poems," *October* 42, 68.

5. Peter Eisenman, "Introduction," *Aldo Rossi in America 1976 to 1979*, ed. Kenneth Frampton (New York: IAUS, 1979) 3. Emphasis added by author.

6. Peter Eisenman, "To Adolf Loos & Bertold Brecht," *Progressive Architecture* (May 1974): 92.

7. Lest this latter device seem absurdly arbitrary, one should compare it to similar strategies of minimalist and conceptual artists like Lawerence Wiener who deployed an aesthetic deskilling of the artist in order to foreground art's framing devices and legitimating institutions.

8. The term "deterritorialized" is from Gilles Deleuze and Félix Guattari, *Kafka: Toward a Minor Literature*, trans. Dana Polan (Minneapolis: Univ. of MinnesotaPress, 1986).

9. Buchloh, "Open Letters," 72.

THE GEHRY PHENOMENON
CAROL BURNS

THE TWELVE YEAR CONSTRUCT established by this conference is an attempt to delimit a present moment in architecture. It is admittedly approximate, particularly with respect to the work of Frank Gehry. Some of the projects that clearly show issues fundamental to his architectural concerns predate this period, and certainly the work of the firm has undergone several important shifts since its founding in 1962. In thinking the present, one is not inclined to argue Gehry's contemporaneity—the work has an undeniable currency. So it is important to remember that the Gehry Residence, frequently underscored as a significant building since its completion in 1978, dates from the very beginning of this time frame. In thinking about Gehry as a particularly American architect, I propose that his work is extremely thoughtful, both visually and culturally, though it is not theoretically driven. The argument, drawn from sources within rhetoric and phenomenology, is not intended as a critical presentation of Gehry's work, but, within the broad realm of architectural thinking, the sources are used to construct a method of discourse consistent, in wide range and in particularities, with the architecture itself.

This is a brief sketch of Gehry's biography: he is sixty years old, born in Toronto in 1929; he moved at age seventeen to Los Angeles; educated at University of Southern California, he first studied fine arts then finished a degree with a major in architecture in 1954; he was a student of city design at Harvard University from 1956–57. Over the years he has developed many famous friendships and collaborations with artists, and has talked openly and frequently about his architecture. Included here are quotations and comments that Gehry has made about the architecture, not only to convey what

he has said but also how he has said it—his figures of speech and plainspoken-
ness. For instance, he has said that he "get(s) . . . inspiration from the streets,"
and is "more of a street fighter than a Roman scholar."[1] This is a situated self-
perception; both identities he uses to describe himself—*more* street fighter,
less Roman scholar—are characters metaphorically placed in particular locations. As examples, they suggest the importance of circumstances in Gehry's
thinking and in his architecture.

My approach to the work of Frank Gehry depends on the notion of topical
thinking. Generally speaking, "topics are the commonplaces of a speech, considerations of a general nature, common to many people and subjects, themes
shared between a speaker and an audience."[2] The word derives from the
Greek *topikos* or *topos*, so that the title of Aristotle's work *Topica* means "of a
place" or "commonplace." Topics are circumstantial: they are local or designed for local application (such as a topical anesthetic); likewise, they dis-
close particular conditions (such as topical allusions).

The obscurity or difficulty of topical thinking stems from its relation to the
art of rhetoric, today considered "an art which has in our times virtually dis-
appeared."[3] Aristotle defines rhetoric as the faculty of discovering the possible
means of persuasion in reference to any subject whatsoever. In rhetoric, a
topic is not only the source of an argument, it is one of the general forms of
argument employed in probable reasoning. Rhetorical persuasion effects certain persons to opinion or judgement or action. The arguments or topics of a
speech and the way in which they are presented therefore depend on the
audience: the moral character, intellectual capacities, state of knowledge, and
emotional potential of those certain persons addressed. Accordingly, an effec-
tive speaker should use terms local listeners can comprehend. "A speech
directed toward a particular community also embraces a specific . . . moment
in the life of that community."[4] Topical thinking is manifestly caught up in
time. "It is neither fixed nor invariant. It works with probabilities,
knowledge that is seemly or likely in certain circumstances, the kind of
knowledge thought of as common sense . . . This accounts for the political or
ethical force of topical discourse."[5]

The presence of this discursive form can still be heard in some of the terms
used to describe an argument in terms of place: the speaker can "take a
stand," "argue a position," or "pose questions." As the particulars of the place
change, so do the arguments. Therefore, argumentation in a mode of topical
thinking necessarily involves invention, and "it is productive in the sense that
it adds by joining and rejoining the places of the speaker and listener together
as they change over time."[6] As a middle term between technical and theoretical thinking, topical thinking has great force in architecture, the most immediate being its comprehension of artifacts.

The notion of topical thinking can be contrasted to its obverse, critical theorizing. As exemplified by the radical, methodological doubt of Descartes,
critical theorizing depends on the solitude or isolation of the native intellect.
The techniques of critical theorizing (in philosophy and geometry, for example) are derived in detachment and produce a set of rules that are technical
and teachable. On the other hand, topical thinking is based in common
opinion, common law, local history, received customs, and language. The
practice of topical thinking (in philology and rhetoric, for example) engages
in practical situations and circumstances, comprising probabilities, not self-
conscious certainties. Critical theorizing lives outside tradition, claims certain-
ty but is also exclusive, and makes a science of things the gods make, the
things of nature. By depending on what lives on and enlivens a cultural tradition, topical thinking is based in observations that are perhaps less precise but
certainly more abundant; it is a science of things that mortals make.[7]

The circumstances of topical thinking are based in the specificities of time
and place. To understand Gehry's work, it is necessary to look at Los Angeles
today. The city itself is a vast and amorphous body, featuring extremely large
horizontal dimensions and lacking any dominant physical order. With a land
take of nearly 500 square miles and a density less than half that of Chicago, it
has the decentralized form of the postindustrial city. Based on automobile
transport and characterized by anonymity, Los Angeles has been called "the
great American commonplace . . . carpeted mile after mile by undistinguished frame and stucco constructions forming a neutral field that is neither
perceived nor remembered."[8] The strand of beach, that physical and social
leveler, marks the line between two horizontal expanses—the undifferentiated body of the Pacific ocean and the plain that was the original site of the
city. The Southern California cult of the body, advocated as early as the 1920s
by Dr. Philip Lovell in *The Los Angeles Times,* is nurtured by a timeless
climate that knows no season. Los Angeles is a city in which cultural history
is short, social traditions pertain to youth or the perpetual appearance of
youth, and geology abridges the sense of the future. Taken together, the conditions of Los Angeles exacerbate the nihilism implicit in all modern culture.
The dissolving void of the ocean, the leveling force of the beach, and the
urban psychology all contribute to an immediate understanding of the
present—meaning exists in the moment and in sensual perception.[9]

Gehry's work is also located in the historical conditions of a culture—growth
and decay. Topics are caught in history, locating moments in time by human
agency. By analogy, architectural knowledge is likewise intertwined in historical time. Gehry has said, "I'm committed to the 20th Century. It's an anti-
Post Modernist thing . . . There is change, and change leads to differences,
and you build on things, and the world is in a progression of some kind,

good or bad, and we're related to the world, therefore we're in that same kind of progression. I'm interested in progress . . . I mean progress in the scientific sense . . . We're tied to a roller coaster and can't get loose." Gehry's work emerges in a particular historical context within Los Angeles. This does not mean that it is "caused" by this context; rather, the work is a way to respond to the received circumstances. In a different state of affairs, different observations, different buildings, would emerge. Just as habits of dwelling exist in time, insights into dwelling types lack meaning if they are not mediated by circumstantial contingencies. In a mode of hypothetical theorizing, typologies escape time; in a mode of topical thinking, constructions exist in time.

The archetypical Los Angeles building—which Reyner Banham calls the "plain plastered cube" and Gehry calls the "dumb box"—is explained by Banham as

> *a firm vernacular basis from which a more conscious architecture can develop. Schindler and Neutra might, almost unconsciously themselves, have put these forms into circulation and imitation. If it is possible to put up a simple stuccoed box in Los Angeles and regard the result as architecture, it is as much due to what the pioneer modernists have done as it is to plain avarice stripping the Hispanic tradition of its ornamental detail. Very large areas of Los Angeles are made out of just these kinds of elementary cubes. They are economically, structurally, and—given the sunshine—architecturally, the local norm and vernacular. Anyone who begins to understand Los Angeles visually has to accept, even celebrate, their normative standing*"[10]

The Danziger Studio-Residence, designed by Gehry in 1964, is an important early project, a simple stucco box. Located at a noisy traffic intersection on Melrose, it is a complex designed to be introverted and fortress-like: double thick stucco walls provide acoustic protection, there are no windows on the street with direct sight lines to the interior, north light comes in from clerestories and popped-up monitors, and the exterior heavy-texture stucco has been left exposed—to collect grime. By accentuating the simple geometric volumes and unadorned surfaces, Gehry amplifies the silence of the dumb box. He said, "I had a funny notion that you could make architecture that you would bump into before you realized it was architecture." This statement clearly betrays the intention to construct a commonplace.

In the anonymous language of American industrially produced buildings, the commonplace is manifest in a variety of ways: inexpensive materials, detailing that lacks technique, standard craft and wood butcher methods of construction, and haphazard accretions both to buildings and to cityscapes through unplanned growth. Gehry uses these qualities to give his buildings the look of being "undesigned."

In a foothill region with an obvious inheritance from the counterculture of the 1960s, the Benson House of 1984 uses raw asphalt shingle exterior walls in the tradition of the California shack builders. Gehry has said, "I like people to have a sort of dialogue with what I do. So even though I often put as much detail work into what I do as anyone, it always appears casual. That's the edge I'm after. For people to see what I wanted them to see, but for them to not be quite sure if it was designed or if it just happened." This is an apparent avoidance of the received role of the architect in favor of the most common custom.

There is an inherent difficulty of working with the commonplace, as Esther McCoy describes, "to isolate the commonplace is not easy; the eye refuses to see it . . . [Gehry] saw how exaggeration can lift the commonplace to an art form. Others perceived this in time—painter Ed Ruscha, for one, drew on repetition of the commonplace."[11] Gehry employs ordinary building

Spiller House, 1980

materials but exaggerates them rhetorically, isolating them through radical placement.

In the Spiller Residence of 1980, for example, corrugated metal and plywood are displaced from their conventional use and joined in exceptional ways. Technical constructions of metal collide with low-tech plywood, combining the machine-made and the handmade. The materials themselves have unambiguous physicality, but they are joined to make ambiguous destabilized space. Applying factory materials to residential buildings confronts normal expectations; making a building of chain link, defining volumes but denying enclosure, seems outright subversive. The Long Beach Aquatic Park of 1976 is a project that includes the first composed use of chain link fencing. The park pavilion started out in mirror glass, which proved too costly. Gehry says that he had long been an admirer of a particular power station with a chain link cover, and then one day an associated landscape architect asked him if he'd ever thought about doing the entire pavilion for Aquatic Park in chain link. Gehry's response was, "Funny you should ask." This may be a simplified story, but it illustrates the notion of an available common ground—the commonality of ideas.

The projects are self-insistent in their Loosian materiality. However, they also bring into focus aspects of the built environment that are typically perceived but not actually seen. These industrially produced materials were not developed nor had they been used with any aesthetic intention (though this has begun to change, due to Gehry and others who have seized his suggestion). By employing common materials in uncommon places, removing them from the neutral condition of the perceptual field to make them the object of attention, Gehry points out our capacity to see the commonplace and shows the richness of things that were not considered rich.

Some different projects that exploit materiality include: the Sheet Metal Crafts Exhibit in the National Building Museum in Washington, D.C., a display of union crafts and standard materials normally hidden within a work of architecture; Rebecca's Restaurant of 1986, where the fascination with the physicality of materials continues when budget constraints are less confining; and the use of lead-coated copper in ensuing projects, including the Schnabel Residence, in which colored copper, applied with rolled edges, makes "scales." This texture corresponds to those seen in different projects by Gehry such as the fish and snake lamps. Overall the textures contribute to an impression of detailing that looks painterly and apparently lacks concern for—even attempts to avoid—neatness. This is part of the a-utopian embodiment of buildings that exist in this world—messy, common, and rich as it is.

The issue of embodiment is fundamental to the temporal or historical character of topical thinking. Corporeality and "situatedness" serve as a reminder of being as being-in-the-world rather than as some theoretical and abstract disengagement. Actually, all theorists confront the problem of making, and every artifact can serve as an object of reflection. On this account, architectural philosophers must construe construction. Embodiment is also brought to our attention in consideration of the public character of architectural settings. In fact, anything that develops out of an architect's subjectivity always encounters, in construction or embodiment, other subjectivities. If critical thinking is a kind of soliloquy, topical thinking is a dialogue. "The study of phenomenology demonstrates that the historical and cultural characteristics of intersubjectivity presuppose corporeality. This doubles the argument on the 'palpability' of rhetorical topics. They are idea/places, figures of thought. Every thought held in common, every topic, is situated concretely. One cannot escape bodily being if thought is to make sense, if it is to be sensed. Topical thinking, as a part of rhetoric, is an architectural way of thinking because it acknowledges the material character of all meaningful artifacts."[12]

Within the context of the issues introduced, Gehry's work will be discussed according to three architectural means of exploring or exaggerating the embodiment of the commonplace: playing with perception, dispersing (or aggregating) building elements and program, and exposing the process of construction. These implicate certain issues that are my topics: the relationship between the subject and the object, the description of figure and ground, and distinctions between originary and original.

PLAYING WITH THE PERCEPTION OF THE OBJECT IN SPACE

The O'Neill Hay Barn, built in the foothill mountains near San Juan Capistrano in 1968, is a simple rectangular volume of corrugated metal on a rigid frame made with telephone poles. The roof is tilted between diagonal corners, which has the effect of putting the building in an oscillating middle ground between the land and the sky. The sloped profile of the form is seen at times against the hills, as part of the profile of the upturned ground against the sky. At other times the metal reflects the sky so that the plane of the roof becomes invisible, disappears into the sky. The building, an autonomous geometrically pure form with obvious affinity to the work of contemporary minimalist sculptors, depends on the viewer's awareness of seeing—an awareness of the role of perception in moving about the site.

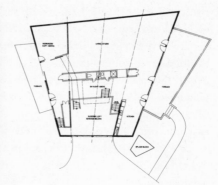

Ron Davis House, 1970–72

The Ron Davis House, built in Malibu in 1972, continues this study of
perspectival illusion within the particulars of a given site. Gehry and Davis
staked out the house together to establish the vanishing points of intended
perspectival illusion, which is the subject of Ron Davis's painting. The house
inflects to both the concerns of Davis and Gehry, the concerns of art and
architecture. It was planned to be a shell, intended to be converted by the
user in a type of collaboration, or infected by the user in a confrontation.
The trapezoidal plan and elevation create an enigmatic form, referring to and
exaggerating the normal perspectival perception of orthogonal architecture.
The roof tilts from a height of thirty feet in one corner to ten feet in the
corner diagonally opposite; windows frame views of the mountains and
ocean, in keeping with the effects created by the walls and roof. The building is based on the circumstances of siting and viewing. In perception, a rectangle is seen as a trapezoid. Through early experience and conceptual interpretation, we deduce that what appears to be a trapezoid perceptually is actually a rectangle visually foreshortened. Indeed, it is impossible to perceive
buildings in the Platonic state, with right angles intact. However, both our
visual perception of a trapezoid and the conceptual deduction of a rectangle
are elements of reality. The Ron Davis House is a conflation of the world of
perception and the world of conception. Gehry has superimposed a perceptual observation onto a physical object, undermining both systems of
knowledge into an ultimately irrational experience.

Gehry plays with the relationship between representation and perception of
objects as an extention of projects first explored in cubism. He designs one-
room buildings because, as he says, they bring him closer to the feeling of a
painter facing a blank canvas. He has worked with the painter and sculptor
Robert Irwin, collaborating on the Easy Edges furniture of 1969–73. Irwin's
work explicitly attempts to isolate perception itself as the essential content of
art as well as the most commonplace condition of each individual's subjective

consciousness. This art begins with things that exist in the environment but
are not looked at, that may seem invisible in their particular circumstances,
yet are nevertheless somehow perceived. Irwin describes his own arrival
through art to topical thinking: "[the last two hundred years of art] have witnessed the loss of the belief in a transcendent content and its replacement first
by a terrestrial subject, and in its turn by the commonplace."[13] Playing with
the perception of the object in space challenges the fundamental and simplistic dichotomy between "the perceiver" and "the thing perceived." This challenge to the relationship of the subject and the object—the self-conscious
individual and the world—is made with the circumstantial material of commonplace existence.

ACCRETION OR DISPERSAL OF BUILDING ELEMENTS AND PROGRAM The program of the architectural addition, often a case of adding to an ordinary or even banal structure, is an important issue not only because it is a common building task, especial-ly for young architects, but also because all
new construction in a city, even on previously unbuilt sites, can be seen as ad-
dition to existing contexts and material conditions. The architectural addition
is inherently conceived in relation to existing local circumstances; it is by
definition topical. This does not preclude the possibility that the addition
may be perceived as primary in itself rather than existing only "in addition
to" something else. One strategy of addition is to attempt to hide the new
work by employing and reproducing the forms and materials of the old building; the other obvious strategy is to design the new without relation to the
existing structure. Instead, Gehry's strategy of addition is to investigate the
situation—the urban context in which he is working as well as the existing
building itself—to discover latent qualities, or potential. These latent conditions motivate the rhetorical stance of the addition so that what is *new*—or
"original" to the situation—participates in the existing construction—or that
which is "originary." This serves first as a release and a criticism of the
received conditions, and then, in a reciprocal manner, a reverberation back
into them. As such, the boundaries between that which is existing and that
which is added become blurred. Similarly, the notion of addition is not
bounded by the actual enclosure of new construction; as it derives from context, so it also serves as a strategy for organizing the entire site. In describing
the ideas he was trying to build with the addition in 1978 to his own house in
Santa Monica, Gehry said, "I wanted to blur the edge between old finishes
and new finishes . . . between real and surreal . . . I was concerned with maintaining a 'freshness' in the house . . . by emphasizing the feeling that the
details are still in the process: that the building hasn't stopped." Both the old

(Top to bottom)
Wosk Residence, 1982–84; Norton House, 1983–84; Sirmai-Peterson House, 1984–86

and the new are made productive; both the originary and the original are aggressive with respect to each other; they both occupy a common place.

The Wosk Addition of 1984 in Beverly Hills, built on the roof of an existing stucco apartment block, is a residence conceived as a collection of smaller-scale pieces that evoke the detail and eclecticism of the surrounding neighborhood. Seen against the skyline, the elements or objects that compose the house occupy the foreground, but have a scale consistent with the buildings that outline the city's profile beyond. Seizing on the American predilection to understand buildings as freestanding objects (posed here as a completely different topic), Gehry's buildings are both object and non-object; the architecture is made of things—positive figures in themselves, and visibly so—that can become latent in their received and constructed circumstances. The Norton House of 1984 is essentially conceived as stacked boxes of a scale made tiny, in keeping with the adjacent beachfront houses in Venice, by stepping them back. The small elevated study structure over an observation terrace clearly recreates the form of a Venice lifeguard stand when seen from the front. But when seen from the street in adjacency to the highly articulated, brightly colored tile volumes of the rest of the house, the study is not a focal object; it is simply one of the many tiny shack structures that constitute the view of Venice. In the urban fabric of Los Angeles, Gehry's buildings are visible but made to vanish into the amorphous pattern of construction. They disallow a singular understanding of the difference between figure and field because they are productive as figures while they endow the field with a productivity by virtue of the instigated interaction. They do not simply define themselves as objects but begin to describe, through their manifold appearances, what Merleau-Ponty calls "unities of sense."[14]

The Sirmai-Peterson House of 1986 represents a change in site strategy in that a missing concept generated in response to urban circumstances is transplanted to an exurban site. Fragmenting the program, making a freestanding house into what can be seen as a village, creates an analogy between the individual and civil society. The person-society analogy is, of course, ancient. In architecture, Alberti, Filarete, and Palladio, to name only Renaissance examples, observed that the house, as an imitation of the way people should live, is analogous or proportional to the city as the embodiment of the way citizens should live. Plato said, "The city is man writ large." Gehry's accretion of autonomous program parts represents the contemporary process of making American cities—the unplanned spread of buildings in urban and exurban environments.

Gehry has said, "What I like doing best is breaking down the project into as many separate parts as possible . . . So, instead of a house being one thing, it's ten things. It allows the client more involvement, because you can say, 'Well,

I've got ten images now that are going to compose your house. Those images can relate to all kinds of symbolic things, ideas that you've liked, places
you've liked, bits and pieces of your life that you would like to recall.' I
think in terms of involving the client." The program is fragmented into parts,
made smaller, reduced. The building elements become an accretion—a social
settlement, a village, a continuation of the ground texture—and make open
spaces that are not civic. A house directly assumes the ambiguous morphology of the city itself. This is disquieting in that it is a simultaneous compilation and fracturing. It is a compilation in the sense that it is an autobio-
graphical assembly for the client; it is a fracturing in that it comments on and
responds to the fragmentation of the extended family, the community, and
urban space.

EXPOSING THE PROCESS   "We all like buildings in construction better
OF CONSTRUCTION   than we do finished . . . The structure is always so much more poetic than the finished
thing." Gehry exposes the process of construc-
tion during renovation to discover existing originary conditions, then uses exposition as a strategy in his new work. In the Gehry Residence the plaster
lath and wood-frame walls uncovered in demolition are left exposed. Using
the same strategy, the Familian Residence project of the same year includes
the first use of exposed studs in original construction. This makes the process
of construction seem interrupted, caught in a fragmentary state of incomple-
tion. An arbitrary moment is clearly marked, but it is surrounded by ambiguity as to whether the buildings are in a process of coming together or coming
apart. The buildings do not aspire to the timelessness of a complete whole;
rather they embody the moment, seeking meaning in an arrested instant.

Gehry Residence, 1978   Familian Residence, 1978

This exposition of parts dematerializes or disembodies the walls, making them unnaturally transparent. However, at the same time, exposing the substrata also endows the walls with a more palpable materiality; the thinness of the walls is constituted by layers of depth. In observing the combination of nonobjective composition coupled with assertive materiality, Rosemarie Haag Bletter states that Gehry's composition is readily comparable to the abstract expressionists' "startling combinations of non-representational forms with a simultaneous emphasis on the tactile qualities."[15] Gehry admits to the association, saying that he explores "the distortion of the rough wood butcher tract house technology . . . into a tool for sketching with wood . . . I guess I was interested in the unfinished—or the quality you find in paintings by Jackson Pollock, . . . or deKooning, or Cezanne, that look like the paint was just applied."

These three architectural means are all used by Gehry to represent a moment in a process, be it in perception, in the process of fabrication, in additions to buildings, or in the growth of cities. They mark moments in time within the city of Los Angeles, within the twentieth century, and within modern architecture. It is a modernism similar to Corbusier's insofar as the evocation of a painterly space and a self-conscious primitivism is accompanied by a sense of social ideals or responsibility. Likewise it is similar to what Stefanos Polyzoides describes in the work of Richard Neutra as "western architectural ideology . . . in that it closely follows economic and material processes in their local development and treats architecture as an expression of those processes."[16] Finally, however, Gehry interprets modernism in his architecture by making strong connections to other realms: commonplace California constructions, including metal buildings, the dumb box, the shack, and the tract house; crafts architecture with its overtly unconcealed woodcraft; the visual texture of a context; practices of painting and sculpture; and certain perceptual and cognitive concerns of contemporary artists.

Here it is necessary to acknowledge a connection to another realm. To address those elements that are explicitly referential, that are figural and directly associational, requires a fish story. In Gehry's words, "Well, it started as a notation of a kind of perfection, unachievable perfection. The fish is a perfect form, and whenever I got stuck, I'd draw a fish in. I had no intention of doing anything more with it." Then, after the break with the Colorcore, "We've been finding this movement. One layer of the fish is movement, the other layer is perfection, that is, if everybody's going to say that Classicism is perfection, then I'm going to say fish is perfection, so why not copy fish?

And then I'll be damned if I don't find reasons to reinforce why the fish is important and more interesting than Classicism. That's intuitive. I don't sit around making up the charge."

The fish is a metaphor, a joint that marks the middle ground of composite knowledge. It is topical in that it is based in the strong opposition between common belief and reflection. Poetic art may be, as Aristotle said, an art of imitation. But it is "not the imitation of humans or objects in nature, not a mirror image nor mechanical reproduction. Poetic figures imitate human possibilities . . . which is why the objects of topical knowledge are neither mundane nor empirical."[17] The fish as a metaphor shows mythical truth, which has no place in objective knowledge—hence the fables, the monsters, and the poetic conceits in the work of architects. In architecture and human life, the marks that signify the temporal and spatial connectedness of things are the locations of poetic truth.

A shift away from the fish as metaphor in favor of classicism itself can be seen in the Loyola Law School project of 1984. The project marks the introduction of a studied use of architectural forms with figural, historical references, in sharp contrast to the early work that is built of layers, floating planes, and material and phenomenal transparencies. These historical references are seen, for example, in the overt form of the chapel or the colonnade suggested by simple, freestanding, cylindrical drums. Gehry said, "It's a minimal kind of postmodernism, if it is. But I would have done it anyway, because of the

Loyola Law School, 1981–84

need to get . . . something that looked like courthouses and that looked like it had something to do with the legal profession, the law school. I had just visited Rome and I got interested in the Roman Forum with all the columns, broken, lying round, but I think that might not have been too easily accepted. So that you have in effect a stage set for a law school."

In the Loyola Law School, Gehry makes an explicit connection to history as a received tradition. At Loyola, what may be typified as historical postmodernism is the arrangement, organization, and manipulation of forms rather than the details of the sources or the stylistic vocabulary. The facade of the main administrative block, broken by twisting stairs, serves as a foil for the simple one-room temple or chapel structures in the campus space it fronts. The hierarchy in this disposition is clear: there is no ambiguity between figure and ground urbanistically because the campus is self-contained within the interior of the block; likewise, there is a singular description of the relation between subject and object, and even the grass landscape is objectified by being sloped and retained by low walls. The columns convey their solidity in remaining upright; more importantly, they are sustained by the stable reading of their external classical reference. The notion of a stage set for a law school is less forcefully composite than the fish as a metaphor, and as it is more literal, it has less poetic potential. It sets meaning in itself rather than enlisting the viewing subject to set and intend meaning. It is a self-conscious irony, which disengages rather than involves the viewer.

Regardless of Gehry's stated source for the Loyola Law School, the shift here reflects, both culturally and historically, the effects of postmodernism on an architect who is manifestly caught up in his own time. In considering this type of historicism, it is also worth remembering the historicizing possibilities of the architectural additions, which are devoid of nostalgic eclecticism in favor of a dialogue between the old and the new. The shift I am describing may not be a shift in direction; it may be the shift of gaze of one who is looking at and participating in the world; however, it is perhaps also a shift in the world that is being perceived. Overall, Gehry's work, in its minimal yet archetypal building forms, documents the futility of the modernist-postmodernist argument. The work proves that neither abstract nor representational forms are exclusively meaningful and that it is possible to evoke the tradition of architecture and its past without resorting to direct quotation.

The poetic connection that appears in rhetorical topics and metaphors is the result of a movement, a descent to "get to the bottom of things." Plato began the great dialogue, *The Republic*, with the word *katabasis*, which means a way down, especially to the netherlands; he wrote, "I went down to the Piraeus," meaning he descended to the harbor, the meeting place of the land and sea. The theme is similar in his parable of the cave; after the ascent to the light from the darkness of the cave, the philosopher is told, "Down you must go," back to the world of the shadows, which is the common source for any insight. For this reason ingenuity—*ingegno*, the mannerist *disegno interno*, or what we mean by "inner sense" or intuition—is equivalent to common sense as the epistemological site of poetic understanding. In returning to the commonplace and descending to fundamental conditions, the figure moving up and down is the scholar who joins different realms together in writing, speaking, and other forms of public rhetoric, including architecture.

Though Gehry expressly disavows any identification with himself as a scholar, it is a fact by merit of his materially, urbanistically, and conceptually joining differences. This is the contribution of the topical thinking offered by Gehry's example in Los Angeles. There are many questions left to be answered in his work. What happens to the architecture when the budgets allow for more expensive materials? What will be the quality of work done in locations other than southern California? Can it lend itself to larger building programs or to high-rise construction? Though the particular circumstances of Los Angeles certainly have supported the emergence of this body of thought, the nature of topical thinking as a discipline argues that it can take place productively in other locations, with the demand that the terms of the argument reconfigure themselves in a continuing responsive dialogue.

Manfredo Tafuri has said that the new tasks given to architecture are paradoxically something besides or beyond architecture. New human tasks are always located in foreign realms, and the boundaries of architecture change as it joins with its tasks in time. This joining is an embodiment of the "liminality of the middle," which directly links the philosophy of topical thinking with the architecture of Gehry. Liminal means relating, or situated at the threshold. Liminality is a sort of seam or joint, marking the ground between territories: architecture and art, *eidos* and *polis*, subject and object, transcendence and immanence. The liminality of the middle describes an approach to difference; it relates opposites by both separation and connection.

> At worst this is a space between, a gap or a divide. Seen at its best, however, it is a figure between, the seam which is a joint or a knot. Understood in experience, such a figure exists in tension, it is knowledge being pulled or stretched. Rhetorical topics stand between a speaker and an audience. Topics are sited at boundaries, in fact they are boundaries. Topics are limits which articulate points of connection. A rhetorical topic is a Janus in space and a January in time, a true coincidence of opposites. The liminality of the middle will be difficult always because it illuminates the greatest differences by inventing points of agreement, which makes it aggressive with respect to the status quo, but also productive.[18]

1. Adele Freedman, "The Next Wave," *Progressive Architecture* (October 1986), 99. Remarks made in interviews by Gehry about his work have been published here and in the following sources: Frank Gehry, *The Architecture of Frank Gehry* (New York: Rizzoli, 1986) and Peter Arnell and Ted Bickford, eds., *Frank Gehry, Buildings and Projects* (New York: Rizzoli, 1985). Ensuing quotations from Gehry will be quoted without reference.

2. David Leatherbarrow, "Review of *Thought and Place*," *Journal of Architectural Education* (Spring 1988), vol. 41, no. 3, 52. The notion of topical thinking as applied here to the work of Frank Gehry is fundamentally based in an elaboration of ideas set forth by Leatherbarrow on the philosophy of thought and place devised by the fifteenth-century Neopolitan thinker Giambattista Vico.

3. Ibid., 52.

4. Ibid., 53.

5. Ibid., 52.

6. Ibid., 53.

7. Donald Kunze, *Thought and Place: the Architecture of Eternal Places in the Philosophy of Giambattista Vico* (New York: Peter Lang Publishing, 1987), 78. In *The New Science*, Vico presents the problem of immanence and trancendence by examining, on the one hand, philologists, who are concerned with culture and that which is made *(certum)* as compared to philosophers, who are concerned with the true *(verum)*. Arguing for a composite truth, Vico maintained that humans may know the truths of only those things they have made *(verum ipsum factum)*.

8. Stefanos Polyzoides, "Richard Neutra," *Los Angeles* (London: Architectural Design, 1981), 67.

9. Gavin Macrae-Gibson, "The Representation of Perception," *The Secret Life of Buildings* (Cambridge: MIT Press, 1985), 2. In particular, Macrae-Gibson discusses the present instant in contradistinction to history as a source for meaning.

10. Reyner Banham, *Los Angeles: The Architecture of Four Ecologies* (New York: Harper & Row, 1971), 17.

11. Esther McCoy, "What You Know, You Question," *Progressive Architecture* (October 1986): 75.

12. Leatherbarrow, "Review," 54.

13. Robert Irwin, *Being and Circumstance: Notes Toward a Conditional Art* (New York: The Lapis Press, 1985), 14.

14. Maurice Merleau-Ponty, "The Primacy of Perception," in *The Primacy of Perception, and Other Essays*, ed. James M. Edie, (Evanston: Northwestern University, 1964), 17.

15. Rosemarie Haag Bletter, "Frank Gehry's Spatial Reconstructions," *The Architecture of Frank Gehry* (New York: Rizzoli, 1986), 29.

16. Polyzoides, "Neutra," 66.

17. Leatherbarrow, "Review," 55.

18. Ibid., 54.

PROLIFERATIONS
HERBERT MUSCHAMP

I HAD A SENSE when I was invited to contribute that I had been asked to take part in a slightly covert baroque enterprise. The text describing the conference seemed to be premised on the view that at one time architecture—and the way it was written about—was embraced by the sheltering if also faltering arms of a canon. There was a coherence of purpose and of language. Then, in the 1970s, there was a kind of Protestant rebellion against the canon, and the result has been a dozen or more years of increasing incoherence, a disunity so extreme as to raise among some people if not the desire for a Counter-Reformation then at least a call for the clarity that once existed.

My task, to survey the entire field of contemporary American architecture, seems to be an exercise in discovering how many American architects can be offended in the shortest possible time, because time does not allow either including their work or going into it with the depth it deserves. In a paranoid moment I might even feel as though I had been set up to make a mess of the subject, because to try to present so complete a picture, even in a hundred hours, is to risk being so incoherent as to represent the symptom for which the cure seems to be searching. But in a sense, what I have been asked to do is journalist's work, to decide what to write about, what is significant, at a time when the choices for subjects are endless.

I am not Charles Jencks, and I have never been all that interested in tracking the weather and its movements through schools, regions, etc. I am interested in variousness, because I think our minds are made to deal with it, and because I like to see the environment reflect what is on people's minds.

Our subject is "thinking the present." Ironically, although I have been asked to focus somewhat more explicitly on the present than some of yesterday's speakers, I find that I must go back somewhat earlier than twelve years in order to render my view of the present with any accuracy.

It seems appropriate to begin an approach to the subject of *Proliferations* by considering first a work from 1974 entitled "Splitting," by Gordon Matta-Clark, an artist who was trained as an architect in the 1960s and whose major work—which for the most part no longer exists except in photographic documentation—adopted existing buildings as raw material. In a series of projects between 1971 and his death in 1978, Matta-Clark used this material to explore issues of form, economics, sociology, and the politics of human settlement in the built world including those issues raised by architectural practice.

Matta-Clark, who was born in 1943, entered architecture school at Cornell in 1962 and studied there on and off until 1969. It is not necessary to rehearse once again the prevailing sensibility in many schools at that time. In 1959, Philip Johnson said, "I think we are getting to a splitting up that is fantastic. I think we are all galloping off in all directions, and all I can say is, 'Here we go.' " But that "we all" was somewhat optimistic on Johnson's part, or at least premature. Matta-Clark was not alone in feeling that this was a period when very little "galloping" was going on; when what was mostly happening was the continuing ebbing away of content from modern forms, leaving little but the perpetuation of a canon for its own sake. We know that Matta-Clark hated the canon, the more he studied it and the more the sixties opened up doorways to information that architecture at that moment seemed unable to channel, much less contain.

Though a small New Jersey suburban house is not, of course, a modern building, we can conjecture on the basis of Matta-Clark's statements that his cuttings were in part an act of violence against the vision of architecture he had been given in school; that he substituted one convention (the suburban house) for another (the modern normative ideal) and went to work with a buzz saw. "Splitting" is not a work of demolition. It was a symbolic act of opening up, parting the walls of a confined space, parting the shell of a norm, to allow the outside world to enter. This was Matta-Clark's way of practicing architecture, his polemical statement that architecture as then practiced was not bringing a world into being but rather that its walls were standing in the way of its realization.

Matta-Clark's "Splitting" was only one of a number of such splittings away from institutionalized architecture that occurred in the 1970s. A 1972 project by Marc Balet (again an individual trained in architecture and a Rome Prize winner in architecture in 1974) is among the first to introduce the idea of narration into the generation of architectural form. Called "Buvete Piu Nervi" (Drink More Nervi), the project is a take off from a 1960s film by Federico Fellini. Here Nervi, the architect as engineer, becomes the embodiment of architecture's appeal to objectivity (even in its poetic aspect); film form becomes a means of representing reason, a surrealistic exploration of a subjective state. The work represents the academy and the impossibility of including certain kinds of information within the architectural container, such as dreams and humor.

A project by Balet called "The Bleeding Arms Hotel" raises a question about which is crazier or more fantastic: the idea of living in a pair of bleeding arms, or the attempt to be "practical" about an implausible vision. In the x-ray plan, architecture's objectivity cuts through and into the human form.

In "Instant City," the pragmatism, objectivity, and utopianism of the modern vision became the subject of parody. Archigram's projects were buildable; this is only drinkable, like Alka-Seltzer the morning after modernism. The demand for "the instant" also speaks of frustration with postponement, an impatience to occupy present ground.

Balet is representative of those who found it impossible to wait for architecture to introduce certain information from within the field itself.

Probably no splitting was more violent in the early 1970s than that of those who abandoned the field to undertake social action on behalf of others whose access to architecture was economically restricted. Robert Goodman, whose work in Boston's Tent City is documented in photography, reminds us that homelessness did not originate in the Reagan years. What also needs to be remembered—Goodman's 1971 book, *After the Planners*, is useful here— is that these splittings away from architecture were usually powered by the perception that architecture itself had split away from the world.

This may seem an odd thing to say of a time that witnessed the large-scale physical realization of the modern vision. It may seem rather more the case that there was a greater congruence between what the profession was envisioning and what the world was coming to look like. Many of the complaints at that time, of course, registered dislike with the way the modern world looked. But I think for many young architects what was most disturbing was a discrepancy between the world projected by architecture and the world outside.

The discrepancy was less one of space than of tense, of time. It was a discrepancy between a generation of architects who continued to view their project as something validated by the future—the omega point in which cities might have rational form—and a younger generation who perceived that this vision was itself a projection of the past. It left the present nowhere, in a vacuum that called out to be filled. In a sense, that filling is what we are looking at this weekend.

Those who split away from architecture are only part of this story. Another part is made by many artists who split throughout the 1970s from other fields—painting, dance, music, sculpture—toward ways of making and thinking and occupying space conventionally ascribed to architecture. Artists such as Siah Armajani and Donna Dennis, for whom the commercial art gallery appeared to be as confining as the architectural profession was to Matta-Clark, turned to the outdoor environment, the space of daily life traditionally occupied by buildings without benefit of the framing device of the art object. For a group like SITE, which began its life as Sculpture In The Environment, architecture was the only true public art.

Whether or not the word "architecture" applies to this work, it is evident that these artists were engaged with architecture, and that their engagement reflected and in some ways magnified an instability with architecture, and between architecture and other fields of cultural practice.

It is possible that much of the work I am about to show could be grouped according to schools, regions, and so on. I have structured this information according to themes, because what remains notable about the present is the continued splintering of ideas and developments that cannot be contained within a neat conceptual grid. I think that it is my fortune to be able to write about things that do not fit with each other. I like architecture that deals with the experience of not fitting, particularly now that many unresolved conflicts have reappeared with the slipping of the feel-good mask of postmodernism.

FRAGMENTATION   Those who were somehow hoping that the Museum of Modern Art's "Deconstructivist Architecture" had killed off this crypto-movement were perhaps chagrined to read that, like a phoenix rising from the ashes of French theory, "The Steel Cloud," had won the competition for a monument to symbolize contemporary Los Angeles.

It may seem a bit like carrying coals to Newcastle to take fragmentation to Los Angeles. Actually, this project is significant in a number of ways, not least for what it says about the problem of talking about architecture in terms of regions and movements. It was designed for Los Angeles by two New York architects, one of whom was born in Cairo to an Egyptian father and an English mother, went to school in Europe, lived in Canada, and studied in

Michigan. The project uses a formal vocabulary developed by Russians, as reconstituted by a contemporary architect who was born in Poland, studied in Israel, and now runs a school in Milan. The vocabulary is also linked to a body of theory vitalized by student uprisings two decades ago in Paris. This is probably what American architecture means today.

Formally, the project demands association with a movement tied to ideas of subversion, of social division, of the collapse of reason. It is held to occupy a position critical of our institutions of power. Nonetheless it was selected, in an exercise in civic boosterism, to symbolize ethnic diversity. This movement has asked that meaning be seen as more than form, and yet the project ideologically can symbolize almost anything at all, except perhaps some older notion of aesthetic conservatism.

I admire this project, as I admired all the projects in the MoMA show; in different ways, they seek the unity of a formal vocabulary to articulate the splitting apart of different kinds of information held in tenuous synthesis by the Modern Movement, and in turn to relate this splitting to the breakdown of faith in Enlightenment ideals. This seems to me a necessary project, even if it raises the critical problems in turn. For instance, the fact that fragmentation, like decentralization in Frank Lloyd Wright's time, may serve merely to mask increasing concentrations of cultural power in the hands of a few. Or that calling attention to reason as a kind of broken toy is a bit petulant—perhaps it is just time to find a new toy that works; or, for that matter, the strong possibility that the Enlightenment project may not be so dead a thing as many suppose. As Richard Rorty has recently observed, "[Contemporary critics of the Enlightenment have] assumed that the terms in which those who begin a historical development described their enterprise remain the terms which describe it correctly, and then inferred that the dissolution of that terminology deprives the results of that development of the right to, or the possibility of, continued existence. This is almost never the case. On the contrary, the terms used by the founders of a new form of cultural life will consist largely in borrowings from the vocabulary of the culture which they are hoping to replace. Only when the new form has grown old, has itself become the target of attacks from the avant-garde, will the terminology of that culture begin to take form."

Like the modern building, the Steel Cloud refers to itself, but instead of being about its structure it is about the process of making that structure, and also about its engagement with the people of Los Angeles. Hani Rashid has described it as a tool for "lifting the horizon" of the city, a city where most of the architecture is foreground. He also sees it as a scaffolding for people and events, so that above the flat, encapsulated environment of the freeway the viewer will observe a social concentration more typical of the traditional city center.

We probably all have a longing for the solidarity of movements. There *are* movements, of course, but they have paradoxically become somewhat private things, some ideas passed around among friends. But movements usually enter the public domain dressed as packages. *The New York Times* wants to publish three of something, whatever it is, so it can report on a trend (the "southwest look," for instance) so that two weeks later it can present something else.

When Mies van der Rohe had his centennial a few years ago, journalistic convention demanded that someone dig up evidence of a Miesian revival. It is not hard to find architects to oblige this sort of thing; you can call around and find three architects who have used travertine or onyx somewhere. And it is not the newspapers or the shelter magazines. The profession has its way of creating packages, and so do the schools. With a museum show, the stakes tend to be somewhat higher, particularly in the case of the Museum of Modern Art, which decided to mostly sit out the 1970s and 1980s in the hope (which I shared) that the postmodern moment would pass.

Like everyone else, I have mixed feelings about the packaging process. The title of my *Artforum* column, "Ground Up," reflects my discomfort in being part of it. Yes, it does flatten things; yes, it does drain away meaning. At the same time, the relentless craving for novelty can perform the critical function of preventing movements from becoming monsters, from becoming the "total package." I like novelty, even for its own sake, because it is a part of colonizing the present, of enlarging the present as a place where contradictory things go on simultaneously, of preventing the past from claiming us.

For me, the MoMA show had all the worst, most flattening aspects of a movement, particularly in the misrepresentation of the work as exclusively self-referential, the cutting away of the connective tissue that gave many of the projects their life: information of physical context, history, theory. These projects were worth seeing precisely because of their receptivity to information of all kinds. Daniel Libeskind, for instance, has explicitly rejected the view of architecture as "an autonomous and self-referential discipline, inventing its own tradition through mute monuments." Instead, he has advocated an approach that "seeks to explore the deeper order rooted not only in visible forms, but in the invisible and hidden sources which nourish culture itself, in its thought, art, literature, song and movement."

Libeskind's use of collage, as in his City Edge project for Berlin, is intended to signify his openness to the information to which we are exposed, information that we ourselves generate and project onto objects in space. I see these forms dealing with the relationship between architecture and other kinds of information, and the breakdown described by Lyotard in the meta-narrative of the speculative unity of all knowledge. Here we have an architecture open to information but claiming to be the crystalline embodiment of all the facts of modern life.

THE BODY

In a number of projects by Liz Diller and Rick Scofidio, the human body operates as a symbol, delimiting where the self stops and the environment begins. But it also becomes emblematic of the porosity between the two. It recasts the autonomous, physical, functional modern body as the contemporary conceptual crossroads of facts and pressures from within and without. From outside come an assortment of messages and demands: what your editor wants; what the architect you are writing about wants; what your children want; what your friends want. Echoing inside the body, these voices are joined by a chorus of dragons, benevolent forces, and mediators. The "Automarionnette" enacts a conflict between man as the measure of experience and man as the item being measured.

"There is good reason," Norbert Elias wrote, "for saying that the human brain is situated within the skull and the heart within the rib cage. In these cases we can say clearly what is the container and what is contained, what is located within walls and what outside, and of what the dividing walls consist. But if the same figures of speech are applied to personality structures they become inappropriate. The relationship of instinct controls to instinctive impulses, to mention only one example, is not a spatial relationship. The former do not have the form of a vessel containing the latter within it."

Diller and Scofidio's Entry Gate for Art on the Beach in New York deals with the body in its role as instrument of control. The design highlights two portions of the body involved with the control process: the eyes survey or command visual control over the environment, and the hand engages in an exchange. We can gain access; the eyes will stop looking at us, provided we are willing and can afford to participate in this exchange with the hand. Of course, we could walk around the wall, but the implication is that we have internalized that message; self-restraint, as Elias described it, long ago replaced external constraint. The wall and the eyes are inside our own bodies.

Diller and Scofidio's Sentinel Building for Art on the Beach is inspired, as the architects acknowledge, by the masques of John Hejduk. Its forms suggest a throwback to the days of court society, before constraint had been internalized. This is what would greet you if you went around the wall without paying. Here, the body becomes even more evident as an armature for architecture; architecture is presented as armor, and as arms for the body, as the way of staking and guarding the body's claim to land. And again we see the hand emphasized: as the gesture of civility; as etiquette that allowed the knight to show he was unarmed and could be approached in friendship; as the seal of acceptance, of the social contract, of the terms of territory. Or perhaps what we see is the weary hand of prisoner beckoning a sign of life from within a cell; the guardian is trapped within the representation of his role. Both readings, and the overlay of both possibilities, are questions the architects are seeking architectural forms to convey; they are central to the issues many critics are confronting in architecture now.

Diller and Scofidio's 1986 project for the Milan Triennale represents an urban window and also suggests medieval armor, but presented in the updated form of electric appliances and electronic media. The helmet is a viewing mechanism that admits light into the interior. The lance is a TV or radio antenna. The project is an investigation of the contemporary city as a place where "modern" self-restraint is only tenuously maintained, where the social contract can break down with the electric supply, cutting off our media extensions and turning us back onto the body's resources.

SPACE

I think Lewis Mumford was correct in warning that the space program is our pyramid, our hierarchy of technology projected into vast space, and is therefore potentially a dubious enterprise for a democratic culture to undertake. And yet it is possible to find visionary work going on within this simultaneously alluring and oppressive structure, work with the potential to turn the pyramid upside down.

Michael Kalil approached NASA several years ago because he took strong issue with the designs being proposed for space stations. He felt that the passage of human life from the surface of the planet to outer space was a transition as momentous as when life crossed the threshold from the primordial ocean to dry land. As a thinker, and perhaps as a taxpayer, he was offended that such an event should be articulated in space stations designed to replicate condominium life in southern California. Kalil secured a contract from NASA and with Jean Gardner proceeded to develop theoretical and practical proposals to structure space and our thinking about it.

Several years ago Michael Sorkin had the idea to write a book about how high modernism was a preparation for habitation in outer space. Kalil sees modernism as a kind of farewell party to euclidean space before we begin to discover space without gravity, without the sense of a horizontal and a vertical. He is asking that, even before living in space is a possibility, we open up a place in the present to begin seeing space in this way. It is now possible and desirable, he says, to make the voyage mentally; it is time to articulate the impact of space on consciousness.

A sequence of seven drawings by Kalil and Gardner represents a conceptual narrative that attempts to align the development of design with the development of the universe.

Like Diller and Scofidio, Kalil is probing the membrane between body and mind to find two ways of looking at a single entity, the language in which he presents his information is closer to science than to art. He is interested in scientifically measurable effects on body and mind of sound, color, shape, and in devising environments that can be modified to produce different effects.

It is possible to see this work as the modern strain of utopianism splitting away into the vacuum of space, with all the problems we are aware of now: flattening of cultural texture, postponement of realization, groveling before the authority of science, the historical *tabula rasa*. I would not mind a Malibu on Mars, and I find myself charmed as well as nourished by the idea that this person lives in a walk-up apartment in my congested city, and wakes up every day to work on his universe of infinite space.

LANDSCAPE

Emilio Ambasz makes use of landscape worth paying attention to right now because of the public alarm about the physical condition of the planet. I am not talking about the meaning of Ambasz's work; I am talking about its significance. Ambasz was utilizing the landscape as a compositional and conceptual element long before the needles began washing up on the beach. Indeed the meaning he ascribes to his work is in some ways opposed to the significance I attribute to it. In the Botanical Gardens in San Antonio, he intends the landscape to refer to a certain idea of timelessness, an idea of the eternal need for shelter. It is an effort to step imaginatively outside history, something I feel quite unsympathetic toward, but my job is to make the significance I see a kind of meaning of its own. It is significant that poison is going into the ground (and rising from it); it is significant that Ambasz's work also points us toward the land. And these points of significance help define a new ground of meaning for a critic to survey.

A young California architect named Warren Wagner has done a project for a sewage treatment plant, for the town of Santa Cruz. It uses an architectural vocabulary that is high tech, but that also draws on the earthworks tradition of artists such as Smithson and Turrell. It is a romantic use of high tech, not only in the idealism of its expression of a desire to contribute to environmental management on the level of infrastructure, but also in its obvious yearning for the romance of the American road—the distant glimpse of farm buildings or oil fields. It turns this approach toward restorative ends; it is a modern kind of romance in which reconciliation with cultural structure outweighs opposition to it. The design is only part of what makes the project significant; the other part is Wagner's Christo-like actions to involve residents, environmental groups, school districts, and civic authorities in the project's realization.

The entire project is dominated physically by an observation tower; this is a project about vision and land, which is what landscape is. It is about vision because it was made by an architect trained in the western tradition of making architecture as a specialized part of visual culture, but the objective of the project is to bring the weight and thrust of that tradition to bear on an area of experience that is not directly connected to visual culture, (though the argument has been made that western visual culture has so detached us from the physical environment as to create the kinds of environmental problems the project addresses). Wagner is using the tools of visual language to bring into focus problems that those tools alone cannot resolve.

A similar idea is operating in a project by SITE for an Ansel Adams Museum in Carmel, California. This is explicitly a work of *architecture parlante*; the forms are carved from the landscape that was the subject of Adams's photography; the entire building assumes the form of the camera that was his tool. The camera frames the subject as well as embodies it. Inside, the museum displays not only Adams's work but also carvings taken from the land, which are made into visual art, though the subject of that art is physical matter.

One of the most interesting landscape projects underway is a collaboration between the architects Henry Smith-Miller and Laurie Hawkinson, the artist Barbara Kruger, and the landscape architect Nicholas Quennel. The commission is to create an art park around the North Carolina Museum of Art. What the group is basically trying to do is to extend post-structuralist theory from culture to horticulture. They are creating a park that is not a stage set of Eden. They call it "Imperfect Utopia," a reference to the original European settlers in the area and also to the industrialized suburb that surrounds the acreage. Their task is to program the space as well as to design it, creating a mix of uses, with planting, art objects, events, even local industry, including industrialized agriculture and the industry of art itself; they hope the work will in some sense represent the theoretical erosion of the nature-culture dualism.

TOURISM　　　　　　　　　The issues raised by architects' occupation of
land are not just ecological. They also involve
conflicts with those who use or have used the
same land, or wish to use it in a different way.

Ours is tourist culture, one that has given itself the freedom to range where it
likes, for study, entertainment, or material or social exploitation. Anthropology offers an approach to other cultures that might help us deal with the
problems of tourism, though anthropology can itself be a form of tourism. I
prefer the word tourism to the word anthropology, as a neutral term that can
carry pejorative connotations but need not.

A project by a young California architect named Laura Gardner is a design
for an exhibition and study center devoted to the culture of a nearly extinct
tribe of Native Americans who once flourished in the Santa Monica Mountains. The project is clearly designed by a modern, western architect who has
conceived a personal attachment to a people who formerly inhabited her
own neighborhood, so to speak. The design reflects the complexity of this attraction and her attempt to make architecture of it.

Modern in form and Wrightian in its use of materials and its relationship to
the land, the building proper is an axial structure oriented to frame a view of
the mountain peak that was the tribe's most sacred site. Outside the building
is an outdoor amphitheater, a performance area based on the sacred circle of
the tribe's religious ceremonies. Gardner does not however pretend that the
design can in any way reconstitute the culture on this site. In fact, the
building's axis penetrates the sacred circle. The design says, in effect, that to
render the substance of this culture in the visual terms of western experience
is to violate its core. Like SITE's Ansel Adams project, Gardner's does not
presume to resolve a cultural problem, in this case the West's awakening to
the loss of its position as dominating the globe. Rather, it uses the means
available to a modern architect to frame the problem.

NARRATION　　　　　　　　A carpet designed by the New York architect Billie Tsien is a visual composition of a
certain elegance, but is no more a matter of
"pure form" than the forms of the letters
that make up the word "narration." The carpet is the evidence of an event—
the suggestion that something has happened in the space defined on the
floor. Someone has dropped a handkerchief on the floor, perhaps accidental-
ly, but it looks like it has had a good workout. Someone was pacing the carpet, weeping, and then left the room. The colors suggest something sinister
as well as elegant. Perhaps the designer had recently attended a performance

of *Othello*. Perhaps we, walking onto this carpet, are Iago, and now we begin to devise our plot.

Le Corbusier spoke of the "plan as generator." Narrative architecture is about the story as the generator of form (and vice versa). Tsien and Tod Williams did a project for the New York offices of BEA, who were the first clients to move into the new Citicorp Building. The architects first saw the space when the building was completed, though they walked off the elevator onto a raw floor slab not yet fully enclosed by windows. The site resembled a new building site on open ground—the contemporary, built-up world's equivalent to a construction site in the dirt. The image that came to them was the construction shack in the Chaplin movie, *Modern Times*, so their design process began with this idea of a construction shack made of cast-off building materials. As the design developed, it followed a narrative of urban development: the evolution of the shack into a small house (the basic office unit); the development of the corridor as a street of small buildings; finally, the growth of a town or village with streets and ceremonial buildings and spaces as equivalent to the town hall, the library, the park.

To respond to this work it is not necessary to know what was going on in the architects' heads. The point here concerns a way of working, a process of making, a process not confined to the manipulation of pure form even though the end product asks to be appreciated on a formal level. In this 1911 cartoon reproduced in Frampton's critical *History of Modern Architecture*, the cartoonist has fun at Adolf Loos's expense by suggesting that his inspiration for the facade of a building came from a sewer cover. In narrative architecture, the architect is the one telling the joke. The building embodies an ambient sensibility—stories from the city, from film, from personal life history, from the experience of the client.

A phone booth designed by Williams and Tsien in collaboration with Mary Miss is about the telephone as a tool and an artifact of narrative. It is hinged, the way telephone conversations are hinged, as an exchange between two storytellers, two callers who depend on that exchange to stitch their time together, and apart. The inside surfaces are meant to be written on by the callers, to leave traces of the voice and its destination, the ear. This project is not about the mechanics of using the phone, nor making space in which to call. It is about the fragile, flexible networks we create to sustain and revise our private social contracts. This is a public phone, and so the architects are experimenting with the flexible barriers between public and private space.

There are several roots for contemporary architectural narrative, the first of which is the building program. More than a decade ago, Bernard Tschumi

and John Hejduk began assigning students projects based on detective stories
and other texts. But even more conventional student assignments offer programs—the home for a movie-maker, the weekend retreat for a business-
man—that are essentially narrative fictions. Narrative architecture looks to
the narrative structure of the program rather than the analytic structure of
functions.

A second source is film, particularly in showing the possibilities for mixing
the tools of a visual medium with non-visual meaning.

A third source is literary theory, simply because literature is where theory is
most abundantly lodged.

Finally, there is the recognition that modernism was itself a narrative, or, as
Lyotard called it, a set of meta-narratives about the liberation of mankind and the
unity of knowledge. Narrative architecture explores that fictional quality not on
the basis of an entire society but rather on the level of individual experience.

Henry Smith-Miller and Laurie Hawkinson designed a house for a couple in
suburban New Jersey who had several young children of their own, and also
had older children (from previous marriages) who sometimes stayed on week-
ends. The town was a wealthy community that had enacted rigorous design
guidelines for new building to maintain the town's traditional character, but
these regulations applied only to the part of the building facing the street.
The architects took these ingredients and turned the house into a story about
the contemporary reconfiguration of family and suburban life. On the street
front is a symbolic facade of a conventional house. Entering the property, it
would be obvious that the facade is just a bow toward conventional propriety,
erected to conceal the untraditional reality of the family's life. The house is in
fragments, with a variety of public and private configurations to articulate the
experience of those who divorce or remarry but keep up continuity with the
past.

In another project by Laurie Hawkinson called "Freedom of Expression
National Monument," the visitor was given a highly conspicuous platform to
yell back at the city skyline. Narrative is about the narrator and the use of the
story to collapse or reshape the world.

The Parasol House by Peter Waldman is a narrative about migration—the migration of architectural forms through an expanding culture, the migration of
Americans through a physically mobile society. It is a six-part sequence that
begins when a couple from the Midwest moves to a small Cape Cod house
in the heart of Houston, Texas. The sequence tells of the couple's acclimatiza-
tion and the gradual transformation of the dwelling to reflect their fantasy of
living in a tropical paradise. By stages, the temporary parasol forms replace

the existing house. It is a conceptual remodeling, a process of transformation as, eventually, permanent cabana forms replace the parasols, and the dwelling has turned from the inside to the outside.

Lars Lerup's No Family House is one of a series of projects he calls "Planned Assaults." His target is the normative—not the modern norm, but rather the vernacular, suburban norm and its power to turn people into extensions of their television sets. The No Family House is conceived to empower a couple and their children to resist being characters in other people's soap operas. Glass Plus may make your windows sparkle, but why not go for a "Fresh Window?" Yes, a nice coat of Pledge will bring out the wood-grained loveliness of your handrail, but why not just liberate the handrail?

The basis of narrative is a sequential structure that progresses from an initial state of equilibrium to a state of disequilibrium, which may be sustained for several episodes or twists of plot, toward a final, new state of equilibrium. Likewise, this is roughly the sequence a critic might follow in the process of interpreting new work.

The initial state of equilibrium occurs before you open the mailbox to find a book in the day's mail with drawings by Lars Lerup for something called "The No Family House." The disequilibrium begins in engaging with the work. See why he made it, how you feel about it, how you feel about an architect working in drawings, working with texts, how you feel about a handrail that takes on a life of its own, do you like the narrative of assault on the family, do you want to bring in psychoanalysis? I have not written about Lars Lerup, so I cannot say I have reached the final state of equilibrium with him, or the point of closure when the significance his work holds is balanced by the time and thought required to write about it.

HOUSING

A project by two New York architects, Lee Ledbetter and Gustavo Bonevardi, is one of a group of projects for infill housing organized in 1987 by the Architectural League in New York. The "Vacant Lots" project was set up to increase social consciousness; to encourage architects to take the initiative, instead of waiting for government to act; and to counteract the image of architects as the willing servants of luxury housing developers such as Donald Trump. The architects were given a choice of specific sites and the freedom to choose their own programs. Several projects are now being built.

The architects of this project chose to design housing for homeless people with AIDS, of whom there are now an estimated 5000–8000. The architects worked closely with a team of social workers and other consultants in designing these units to allow those with AIDS to remain living in their neighborhoods after losing their homes. They provide private accommodations, public rooms, space for medical consultation, a garden.

The project is significant not only as a design but also in recognizing that AIDS is not just a medical or a social crisis but also a cultural one. If you recognize the cultural impact of AIDS, it may not be enough to send a check, write your congressman, or attend a benefit. These architects felt moved to devote that part of themselves—their work—that connects them most actively to their culture. They are not writers, dancers, or musicians; they have chosen to exercise their responsibility as architects.

The Madhousers are a group of architects who prefer to remain anonymous, since what they do is illegal. They are based in Atlanta, and to date they have erected approximately fifty-five huts, of which three or four have been demolished. The group does not think theirs is the best solution to homelessness; also they are aware that this solution would not work in many cities, though it happens that Atlanta has a large amount of vacant wooded land. They do believe that for some of the roughly 200 homeless people they have housed, using one of these huts has provided enough economic stability for eventually affording an apartment.

I think it is possible to look at information like this and not interpret it in terms of guilt and anger, though I confess that I did feel angry to hear Michael imply that there is something the matter with the idea of hope. Perhaps it has never occurred to him to make the connection between the word hope and something he has experienced in his own life. Perhaps that is why he has such trouble with the idea of meaning also. In any case, for many of my generation, giving up the idea of hope is a luxury, an assertion of privilege, well beyond our present means.

Auden wrote, "Then, much as we should all like to, none of us can preserve our personal planet as an unsullied Eden. According to our time and place, unpleasant facts from the world we all have in common keep intruding, matters about which either we are compelled, against our will, to think or we feel it our duty to think, though in such matters nobody can tell another what his duty is."

BEAUTY I am very grateful these days for the word "beauty." It is simple, imprecise, and somewhat empty, but in a way that invites being filled up with a new sense of its intelligence. It is formalism's ancestor as well as its heir, an idea formalism made easy to forget. And it is easy now to think that beauty is somehow not enough, that objects are incomplete without theoretical texts. When I look at Stephen Holl's work, I am sorry that this is the case. I feel I am in the presence of objects complete in their beauty; that the texts the architect has felt compelled to attach to them are a bit like millstones, or bitter pills I resent being asked to swallow.

I am aware of Friedrich Nietzsche's objection that "to experience a thing as beautiful means to experience it wrongly." And I am aware of the need some architects feel to distance themselves from formalism and from the emptiness of postmodern ornamentation. Zaha Hadid has said, "We don't want to be cake decorators." Actually, it is not so easy to be a good cake decorator, and it is particularly difficult to decorate a cake in a new way. Much of the power of those incredible drawings of Michael Graves from the 1970s is simply that they were a new kind of beauty. Zaha Hadid's drawings have been exercising a similar power in the schools in recent years.

I do not mean to suggest that theory is wrong, or that it is not an integral part of a lot of exceptional architecture. Nor do I mean to place beauty at the top of a hierarchy of ideal attributes. Such a hierarchy contributed to formalism's depletion of modern architecture's vitality. Rather the idea is that form now has the particular beauty of a fragment, almost a ruin, not the mystery of an essence.

My sense of Holl's significance as an architect is not enhanced but limited by the invitation to see his projects as advance messengers for a larger and more theoretical vision of the contemporary city. I am not persuaded that the city stands to benefit from architects's plans that claim to allow "the modern soul to emerge" (as Stuart Wrede wrote). I do not think that soul is awaiting the permission of architecture—I do think it thrives as much as the old soul did on beauty.

I have a problem with the writing of urban prescriptions. I am not sure that for architects—or for artists or critics—to dictate the physical form of "the city" is not to perpetuate the kinds of hierarchy—of knowledge, of class, of sensibility—that oppose what the contemporary soul is.

If beauty is a problem, it is partly because beauty is itself a splitting away from the modern synthesis of abstract form and progressive social content; beauty must long for content, like the divided body in Plato's work.

Yet my inclination is to read Holl's Edge of the City project not as an attempt to make his forms urbanistic in a sociological sense but on the contrary to set psychological limits on sociological imperatives. It is his own soul seeking to limit the expectation that to be beautiful today is to be sociologically insensitive. Happily, he has let holes in the wall to let ideas blow in from outside.

I cherish architects who are queer for beauty, not in response to beauty as
the only or the best thing but in response to anyone who is really good at
something—anyone who pushes it, or seems to be led even against their
will.

Frank Israel is an architect whose feel for the beautiful has benefitted from his
move from the East to the West Coast. Californians, I know, are tired of
being treated as beautiful and dumb, yet in Israel's case the move was symbolic as well as geographic; it freed him from a tendency to rely on extrinsic
ideas of history and theory, though, of course, the work is linked to those
ideas through the history and theories of form itself. The Gillette Studio, a
New York interior that Frank began during his early residency in Los Angeles,
references Barragan, photographs of whose work, exhibited at the Museum
of Modern Art in New York in the mid-1970s, had an enormous impact in
authorizing architects to push aside strategies of sociology and theory in order
to practice beauty as a form of intelligence. Bernard Tschumi says that whenever he gives a talk about La Villette, someone in the audience inevitably asks
him why the follies are red. I doubt that anyone asks Frank Israel why the
wall in Propaganda Film Offices is red; it is red because Frank loves the way
it looks and has situated it in a context so it stands out and looks its best.

Israel has adopted a relaxed attitude about whether or not he is a postmodern
architect. If you wanted to put him in the package, there is probably some
justification for it, but to me, he represents the best kind of freedom
postmodernism introduced. He is not sacred about history, about classicism,
about essence. He is happy to steal any vocabulary—from Wright, from Gehry,
from Japanese traditionals. It is almost impossible to visualize what a Frank Israel
building looks like. It is a completely contemporary kind of beauty, one that
wants to remake constantly, rather like Madonna. Its hallmark is its independence from formula, including the formula that one must be consistently
original.

THE SURFACE   We know that with architecture we are dealing first with a class of material objects in
space, which are related to certain production
methods as Robert Gutman has analyzed in
his book, *Architectural Practice: A Critical View*. But we also know that as students of architecture and consumers of contemporary culture we are dealing
with a class of images with which we are furnishing our minds. This class,
too, has its methods and systems of production; I am a cog in a few of its
many wheels. I am part—or at least my mailbox is a part—of the joining of
two systems, the point of exchange where that part of architecture that deals

with the manipulation of images connects to that part of the media that filters
and organizes their distribution.

There is a lot of moralistic sermonizing that takes place about the over-
reliance on the published image, on the power of the photograph to kill the
place. There are good grounds for such complaints. The problem is, what do
you do about it? Jean Gardner is quite persuasive in making the case that the
dissociation of architecture from place began centuries ago, when the use of
visual perspective supplanted sacred association as the means of distinguishing
a place from its surroundings.

Helmut Jahn's architecture is disliked by many because it seems to be shaped
by marketing pressures and the media. People used to complain that buildings rarely looked like their photographs; now the complaint is that they
look altogether too much like their photographs. It is useful to ask why the
forces of marketing should be considered any less suitable an authority for
design than the forces of industrial production that authorized the modern
canon. Ours is, after all, a culture and an economy in which marketing has
been supplanting production as an economic force. This new era, to
paraphrase Mies, is a fact. It exists irrespective of our yes or no. I do not care
for Jahn's architecture, but I think that some ground for criticism must be
found other than *its*—as opposed to our—involvement with surface.

Jahn seems to be a transition figure in the passage of power from production
to distribution. The passage reaches its destination in the work of Arquitectonica, which is perhaps one reason why people are less disturbed by it.
Arquitectonica's buildings really know how to smile for the camera. They
know a good photo opportunity because they are one. The great joke about
the Sky Patio in Arquitectonica's Atlantis Building is that the cut through
the building exterior reveals more exterior. Beneath the surface is more surface. It is like the joke about the real tinsel beneath the tinsel; at least it has
the power of conviction. It allows imaginative inhabitation of the flatland
world of the media, the TV screen, the glossy magazine; it seems no more
spurious than the modern building that allowed imaginative living in the
world of technological production.

I am uncomfortable writing about buildings I have not seen first-hand; but I
am writing for an audience that most likely will not get to visit these buildings; and it is not necessary to do so in order to furnish our minds. Architecture is perhaps the most public of the arts, and yet I think that much of its
public life is about the mental furnishing made possible by images.

I think a photographer like John Margolies has enormously enriched our
sense of architecture by traveling around the country to photograph buildings
that are rarely seen firsthand. Through his images, these obscure buildings

have become a distinctive part of architecture's public life—they alter the way we see. I am sympathetic to an architecture that embodies an awareness of this process. For instance, the hotels of Morris Lapidus were consciously designed to appeal to people who loved Hollywood musicals.

Since Walter Benjamin first wrote about "The Work of Art in the Age of Mechanical Reproduction," a considerable vocabulary has grown up for talking about this kind of work. I have used that vocabulary myself on occasion, but I also want the right to use very different kind of vocabulary, words like, "You look fabulous!"

MEMORY AND HOPE The last project I want to mention is by an architect, somewhat older than the others, who is a partner in a large firm. I think the project is so exceptional that it does not fit into any category easily and so is not out of place in a mixed survey like this one. The Holocaust Museum by James Freed, now under construction just off the Mall in Washington, would command attention on the basis of its program alone, even if it were less remarkable a work. It is important because of the events it commemorates, because of the significance of those events in the history of reason, and because of the building's contribution to that history.

It is a considerable departure for Freed, who has never accepted the erosion of the Modern Movement as inevitable. Yet he has devised for this building a vocabulary that differs radically from the canon he has adhered to over the years. This is a building in which the denotations and connotations of forms take precedence over their appearance.

Two kinds of vocabulary collide in this work. The first, most evident on the exterior, borrows from official or state architecture—the architecture of the "Empire of Reason" that shapes official Washington, and that denotes our roots in the Enlightenment of eighteenth-century Europe. But he has not used this vocabulary uncritically; the building tells how the official masks of elaborate ideals can veil inner horrors. The entrance facade to the building recalls the historicism of postmodernism, and while that satisfies the requirements of the Art Commission who must approve the design, it is also a critique of postmodernism's complacent deployment of classical manners to cover up inner life. The other vocabulary operating in this building is also drawn from the history of architecture, but it is an unwritten history, the history of the ghettos and the death camps that, as Freed makes plain, were the handiwork of designers. People designed the gates to the camps, the observation towers, the shutters on the windows, the ovens, the oven doors, and the metal bands around the ovens. The interior of the building, particularly the central spine Freed calls the "Hall of Witness," is made from these forms.

Freed does not accept the Frankfurt School idea that the Holocaust was a consequence of Enlightenment ideals. He believes in the viability of liberal culture and in the power of modern architecture to continue to serve liberal ideals. But the design also reflects the sense that the Holocaust continues to put pressure on those ideals. There is a large crack in the wall in the Hall of Witness, the roof trusses are warped, and the metal bands that suggest the containment of evil behind the walls could also connote the need to hold together a crumbling belief in reason.

For all its departure from Freed's previous work, I see this as a very modern building, not just in the visual terms of the Modern Movement, but in freely borrowing from many different approaches architects have taken to coax a modern world into being for more than two centuries: *architecture parlante*; radical classicism; proto-modern industrial and vernacular forms; canonical modernism; even, in the roof trusses, the fragmentation of work by architects of a younger generation.

This modernist use of history serves an urgent present need to retrieve from the past an event that time has not buried, an event that in fact looms larger in consciousness with the passing decades of shock and denial. It seems more a part of "thinking the present" as each year one is struck by how recent and unresolved an event it is. The building is being erected to mark the extinction of Jews and to provoke a consciousness of the possibility of a recurrence. It retrieves the past and demands a place for it in the present, in hope that such horror can be lodged in the past forever.

CONCLUSION

I said earlier that it is the writer's business to make meaning out of significance and I would like to conclude with a word on what I make of the significant elements I have picked out to present. I have been writing about a conceptual restatement of the modern attempt to engage the creative process in the continual redrafting of the social contract. It is something that is no longer being worked out by a dialectic between the future and the past—a past of arbitrary individualism with its echoes of authority concentrated in kings and God, a future collectively planned and realized. Rather, it is happening in the rise and collapse of phenomena in the present, as the mind observes it happening and thinks it into happening. In the present, collectivity does not look like something achieved by consensus, because it no longer looks with faith to a future in which consensus has been imaginatively attained.

One wants to keep a vision of architecture as evidence that intelligence and action are being brought to bear on the widest possible range of human experience. One wants to see one's experience of the world reflected in an activity that is concerned with making and remaking the world—perhaps because it fulfills narcissistic needs, or perhaps because we have only fleetingly glimpsed an environment not dominated by a few. But that does not mean that any particular building, or any particular architect, need reflect everything in the world.

It is enough to make a beautiful building, it is enough to create a shelter for a homeless person, it is enough to sit in a New York apartment hatching inspired, wild man theories about the meaning of the venture into outer space. None of these elements are exclusive. It is fine to take as many as you like, to pick them up, drop them, and pick them up again from a new point in present time. For me, as a writer, architectural culture is about making speculative connections and juxtapositions between these and other elements as they unfold in the present, influenced by many factors and contexts over which architects have little if any control. But it is not necessary that architects themselves always make these connections, nor that they all be made in any one building.

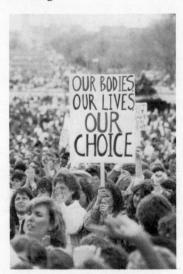

Pro-choice march in Washington, D.C., held the same day as the *Thinking the Present* conference.

What one wants, to paraphrase Frampton, is a kind of critical regionalism of the mind—a resistance to the prescription of architecture as a total package; a willingness to block out certain kinds of information and desires in order to get a project done; a willingness to collect scraps of information without placing upon them the burden that they all add up to a whole. One wants texture as well as structure.

We know from urban life that reason alone cannot make a social contract, cannot define the relationship of the environment to the self. It takes more than theory to see them as two aspects of life. I think the social contract is framed by nothing but creativity, bringing out from within ideas of all kinds, including, periodically, silence.

ARCHITECTURE, DEVELOPMENT, MEMORY
HAL FOSTER

I AM NOT AN ARCHITECTURAL HISTORIAN. I say this partly as an excuse and partly to get permission to speak speculatively—in a way that most people schooled in a professional language do not often speak. Cultural critics often regard contemporary architecture as if it were somehow isomorphic to economic forces. Although I, too, will sometimes treat it here as a simple inert object, what in fact interests me is its discursive complexity or instability.

The Russian Revolution confronted artists with the potential anachronism of the category Art. So now, in a very different way, advanced capitalism confronts architects with the possible obsolescence of the category Architecture. But one can read this development otherwise—as a mandate to think the "refunctioning" of the discipline. (For all its merits, it must be said that this symposium did not pursue this possibility.)[1] The first part of my text touches on the present conditions of such a refunctioning; the second part concerns the emblematic role of architecture in historicist models of history. It is presented here largely as it was given: a few notes, some questions, no single argument.

I want to begin with a general remark about criticism that is especially important for architectural discourse. For me the concept of criticism is bound up with the concept of the public sphere. Now whether one regards this sphere as historical or heuristic, criticism depends on it. In certain ways the two forms, the institution of criticism and the notion of the public, are coeval aspects of the same bourgeois cultural revolution. Of course, this revolution was stopped short when other groups—initially other classes—demanded that the rights and representations of the bourgeoisie be made truly public, truly open to all. This demand continues in different ways, and it is only in this form, in the many counter-publics of the present, that one can speak of a public sphere at all. (For the most part, the old public sphere has gone the way of spectacle—to the point of our corporate-state-media sphere). Yet, institutionally, criticism has not proven very able to sustain these counter-publics, to articulate residual and/or emergent interests alternative to dominant ones. Nor has it proven very able to pressure architecture, its institutional support, to do so. By and large it has accepted its own default—even embraced its erosion as a site of analysis and alternative. Too many architectural critics are bagmen for the boys downtown.

If this sounds reactive at best, paranoid at worst, it is. And that is my second general point about criticism today. Critical culture depends on political culture, and our political culture is reactive in its anxiety about the present; the mainstream is pledged against the innovative, the other. In such a climate criticism cannot help but be reactive too, and it is; when it is not simple ratification, criticism is steeped in resentment, trapped in negation, severed from affirmation. And I mean affirmation that is critical, not celebratory, of the status quo—affirmation that releases new modes of thought and action as well as rescues repressed modes in cultural, social, and political life. There is a great atrophy of this annunciatory criticism today, and practice atrophies with it.

What does all this mean for contemporary architecture? For one thing, it is rarely received as a practice of public concern. How often do the journals present architecture as a civic issue of civic participation? And how often, when it is so discussed, does the subject involve everyday building—and not this designer-design or that architect-personality? When architecture is received as an activity of public concern, this public is rarely captured in its condition of conflict and contestation; it is seen instead as a supine statistic. As a result, architecture and public become disjunct; one effect is that the public aspects of architecture are treated as reified quotients. Relegated to categories like ersatz atriums and puny plazas, meaningless monuments and monster malls, these public quotients of architecture are compensatory; they serve, like most public art, as pathetic substitutes for spaces of public appearance. (At least such nineteenth-century precedents as the department store and the grand boulevard possessed a phantasmagorical wonder that provoked a reflexive, Baudelairean subculture; so far the malls have given us *Dawn of the Dead*.) A nuisance to powers that be, they are used only by the homeless, who are harassed there. (The rest of us are merely surveyed.)

Another corollary effect of this discursive separation of architecture and public is that architecture is regarded primarily as an individual practice—again, in terms of this design by that architect-personality or this project by that megalomaniac-developer. Not much critical consideration is given to the social complexity of architecture (e.g., the impact of an office building on

the community of its site or the psyches of its users) or even to the actual
practice of building: not just grands projects like the mini-city spectacles of a
Baltimore waterfront, but the workaday architecture of new urban villages,
office parks, and governmental buildings. As far as I can tell, such activities
are rarely acknowledged by architectural discourse; they are shunted into
other categories (Business, Real Estate, Arts and Leisure). And this, I submit,
is an extraordinary mystification in which architectural criticism, theory, and
education all generally participate. The powers that be (the Philip Johnsons,
Donald Trumps, and Ed Kochs in your megalopolis) could not devise a more
perfect ideological mask than the one we produce and reproduce daily in the
course of our own practices as architects, critics, and teachers—even (or especially) when we think we are at our most theoretically subversive. (My tone
may suggest that these developments are new, but in fact they comprise the
present state of an historical process—the architectural/urban vision of state
capitalism—punctuated by such famous figures as Baron Haussmann and
Otto Wagner, Albert Speer and Robert Moses, Philip Johnson and John
Portman.)

On this score, architectural criticism is an easy target, but it is not my only
one. Architecture in the academy also participates in this mystification. It
does so simply when it excludes or neglects certain mundane architectures,
political processes, or social groups. In my limited exposure to architectural
conferences and academic critiques (the first often gladiatorial, the second always sadistic), these things are often held to be beneath contempt or at least
beneath interest. Again, I speak as a layman, and for the layman two figures
have come to dominate the field: the developer-architect and the academic-
architect. According to this view, architecture has become subsumed by
development, on the one hand; on the other hand, it has become rarefied in
the academy. This is cynical, perhaps overly so, for there are points of resistance and renewal in both arenas. But this process of reification and rarefaction in architecture cannot be denied. How is this located historically? Does
it begin with the split between architecture and engineering—a split that
rarefies the practice of the former as it allows the logic of the latter to
dominate? Does it derive from the ambiguous position of architecture, as the
most practical or worldly of the arts, in the modernist projection of formal
autonomy? This will to autonomy was also part of the bourgeois cultural
revolution, but to a great extent its critical charge is now void. Indeed, to a
great extent this will to autonomy allowed the rarefaction of architecture in
the academy that in turn abetted its reification in development. In any case,
exactly how this happened, exactly how the developer-architect and the
academic-architect were produced, I cannot say. I can say, however, that one
way to respond to these twin figures is to produce another dialectical pair: as

opposed to the developer-architect, the political architect; and as opposed to the academic-architect, the counter-disciplinary architect.

Now what might this first creature, the political architect, be today? Well, for example, rather than develop homeless shelters as part of a zoning variation or a building deal (as a developer might), an architect could work to expose the architectural preconditions of homelessness—maybe not in building, maybe not in drawing, maybe outside the discipline as it exists today. But to present schematic shelters to the homeless or to reimagine the house type altogether—the first as a conscientious salve, the second as a compensatory vision of grandeur—is not enough. Instead an architect might reveal the production of homelessness as an effect not only of certain policies (regarding welfare, housing funds, and so forth) but also of certain architectural/urban assumptions. Now, perhaps, I sound naive rather than cynical. For what happens then to architecture? Might it not just become politics or economics or sociology? In part. But what is architecture now, what has it ever been? And such an analysis is not irrelevant to sophisticated discourse. Deconstructivist architects argue that both premodern and modern architecture are mired in a metaphysics of presence—of the shelter, of the home. If this is true, an anti-foundational critique of such architecture might make the homeless its subject. So, too, it might consider the *unheimlich*, the uncanny. Both these terms exist at the limit of architecture. Architecture enframes. Abjected, the homeless are pushed outside the frame—and so challenge it. The same is true of the uncanny: architecture rarely allows for sensual intuitions of space and structure; what might happen if it entertained unconscious ones? Indeed, what might a psychoanalytical architecture be?

What about the figure of the counter-disciplinary architect? I pose this figure in opposition to the rarefied academic-architect, and here I appeal to a post-structuralism that is not so active in architectural discussion today, at least as this discussion centers on deconstructivist architecture. Now, we can argue whether deconstructivist architecture is truly deconstructive of architecture, or true to the methodology of deconstruction; clearly architecture is an important site for an inquiry. But at one point we must ask where such architecture stands in relation to the general rarefaction-reification of the discipline today. For example, it may well address the metaphysical assumptions, the humanist subject-positions, of architecture in a Derridean sense. But does it engage the aspects of the discipline in the Foucauldean sense? Unless it does, I am not sure how fully critical, even deconstructive, it can be. I mention Foucault—and I mean here the Foucault primarily of *Discipline and Punish*—to suggest one way that a counter-disciplinary architecture might proceed. I do not apply Foucault and company's ideas as a manual, but use them to think the disciplinary aspects of architecture. I use "disciplinary" in the sense

of how architecture constructs its authorial subjects and trains its practitioners
as architects (in relation to other discourses and practices, of course, but also
in the university, even in apparently nondisciplinary curricula and projects);
and disciplinary in the sense of how architecture constructs its recipient subjects, and trains our spatialities and temporalities, our bodies and minds, our
conscious and unconscious activities. In short, the point is not so much to
contrive (say) anti-panoptical projects, but to consider whether or not architecture can be thought outside a system of a surveyed space, outside a
regime of a disciplinary gaze, outside an order of regimented bodies, outside
a time-space of compelled circulation (the flow of people, goods, information, money)—in short, to think architecture in terms of its technical,
microphysical effects on our bodies and minds.

A question here in passing: For Foucault the gaze historically produced in different architectures and inscribed in different subjects is sexually indifferent.
Is this so? Can a critical architecture today afford to think that it is so? And a
personal aside as well: Recently, I have become interested in typological
developments. Late last fall (1988) I was in Seattle, my hometown, for an architecture conference. As if to compensate for its evermore dense
downtown, there is a spacious new mall, and it struck me as a weird inversion: an initially urban type, the department store, first developed into a suburban type, the shopping center, and now returned to an urban setting. This
inversion—it has happened elsewhere too—is troublesome, because the suburban mall is presented as a primary form of public urban space. It is accepted
as a space of public memory, too, which makes it even more problematic, for
in such spaces the history of place is consumed as spectacle. In Seattle, this
means the use of a Northwest Coast Indian design abstracted as a general
logo for the mall.

A few weeks later I was in San Francisco, where I saw a further development
of the mall type called The San Francisco Emporium. Here not only is the
suburban mall transplanted to the city, but the horizontality of the shopping
center is rotated back to the verticality of the department store. Picture a
structure that is a spiral a la Guggenheim Museum: the floors appear as bands
around a central abyss. On every floor, one is forced to stop, to walk by
stores, and to pick up each escalator. Granted, I was there in the Christmas
frenzy, but I have never experienced such architectural delirium; it is beyond
the vertigo registered by Fredric Jameson in the Portman Bonaventure Hotel
in Los Angeles. Apart from the subjective effects, people are positioned in
this emporium as particles in a wave chart, surveyed and directed strictly in
terms of flow, a flow that appears free because random. (Do men and
women, children and adults, inhabit this flow differently? Do designers account for such differences?) Meanwhile, the stores, long eroded within by

the protean commodity, are now eroded without by the demands of circulation. There is minimal definition of each store; in fact, the structure has an almost televisual transparency that attests to the present transformation of architecture in our social regime of spectacle surveillance. (Indeed, a primary architectural experience today is an image of your own body in a monitored
space—an elevator, an apartment lobby, a museum, etc. The limits of architecture are continually extended, dissolved, redefined in this way—caught
between the inertia of our bodies and the acceleration of everything else.) In
the emporium there are simply stores on levels in bands around the central
abyss. If for Walter Benjamin the department store was a hell in the phantasmagoria of the nineteenth century, this place is a contemporary purgatory.
Your money or your life. You shop or you jump.

Now for architecture to be critical in the counter-disciplinary sense that I
want to develop, it must reflect on its own role in techniques of power. I am
confident there are such investigations under way. Here, however, rather
than speculate, it might be useful to consider, albeit abstractly, the premises of
critical programs already in place. Often such programs are conceived in
terms of an oppositional architecture. This immediately raises the famous
question of Aldo van Eyck: How to pose an architectural counterform in a
urban society without form? I used to think this was a provocative paradox,
but it now strikes me as a misbegotten opposition, one that may debilitate
more than support a critical practice. For the notion of a "counterform" suggests that there is only an outside or inside to our social dynamic, a dynamic
that the notion of "a society without form" suggests we cannot really know.
But our capitalist social dynamic can be known; it may be difficult to represent, let alone resist, but this is not *a priori* an impossibility, at least as long as
one does not oppose an outside to an inside. This opposition is now
deconstructed—less by Derrida or Deleuze, Peter Eisenman or Bernard
Tschumi (though they help us to think it) than by advanced capitalism. And
yet it still seems operative in critical thought, in architectural thought, where
it is reproduced in such a way as to constrain theory and practice to one of
two positions: either an inside position, such as the model of a "collage city,"
which is often interpreted as a curatorial, even commemorative approach to
modern development, or an outside position, from which one can only im-
pose a more or less utopian model onto the city. (This latter position often
takes the form of a will-to-monumentality in modernism and a will-to-mar-
ginality today.) In the inside position, one tends to "relate to the forces of the
Grosstadt like a surfer to a wave" (as Rem Koolhaas has put it); and in the
outside position, one seeks to transform the city according to some totalist
logic or some private dream. When such a transformation was partially possible, it tended to tear up the city—to fragment it all the more. And now,

when it is much less possible, it serves to reinforce the marginality of the architect, a marginality that many architects today fetishistically embrace as if architecture were now only sustained authentically through tokens of its "loss" or "impossibility."

My point here is not that the notion of an oppositional architecture should be surrendered, but that its terms must be rethought. It might be that the notion of a critical architecture is problematic too, but for the opposite reason: not because it projects a mythical outside to the social field (an outside that is then either heroically overcome or whimsically embraced), but because it assumes too much the field that it seeks to transform. By this assumption it becomes closed to the very historical changes, to the very innovations in spatialities and subjectivities that it might otherwise articulate to radical effect. Such articulation, by the way, is my ideal: an architecture that, rather than disciplines spaces and subjects to a synchronic calculus of design and technique, recovers residual spatialities and subjectivities and articulates emergent ones—an architecture that would, in effect, set architecture in motion in a way sensitive to the nonsynchronous nature of our historical experience.

How is such a model different from an architecture of resistance? Maybe this is to hypostatize another term (as perhaps I did above with the notions of "oppositional" and "critical" architectures), but "resistance" seems to stake a defensive posture; that is, it tends to forfeit the annunciatory possibilities of practice. In short, like "opposition," "resistance" must also be rethought; what this might mean can be suggested by a very important model of an architecture of resistance, the model of "critical regionalism" proposed by Kenneth Frampton.[2]

Frampton begins with an opposition of universal civilization (rationalist, "technophilic," capitalist) and regional culture; the first is pledged to appropriative expansion, the second to cultural difference. Rather than trust in the innovative aspects of new capital or in the traditional aspects of old cultures, he advocates a dialectical engagement of the one by the other, whereby each in effect criticizes and corrects the other. It is a strong concept, one that, articulated in the work of his cited designers (Alvar Aalto, Jorn Utzon, and Mario Botta), can approximate the sort of architecture I advocated above—an architecture sensitive to the complexities of residual and emergent spatialities and subjectivities. But unless one lives in a relatively homogeneous society (as did or does the Finn Aalto, the Dane Utzon, and the Swiss Botta), it may be difficult to act upon today. For the principle of "critical regionalism" is tied to a problem that may not still be our own, not entirely anyway. A primary theoretical source for the notion of "critical regionalism" is a 1961 essay called "Universal Civilization and National Cultures" by the philosopher Paul Ricoeur. In 1961—after the liberation wars of the 1950s and before the neocolonial conquests of the sixties and seventies (that is, before the First World's re-penetration of the Third World to supply its labor fund and marketplace)—Ricoeur could still look to the new postcolonial configuration of the world with optimism. In such a moment of release it was possible to project a genuine "dialogue" between worlds, to insist on the resistance of the regional; twenty-eight years later it has become much more difficult. This is not to say that mono-civilization is an accomplished fact, that capitalism has penetrated everywhere. (I have less and less sympathy for the apocalyptic models of contemporary cultural criticism that speak of a universal West or a hyperrealistic world; often such criticism is simply another refusal of differences.) But it is to say that relations of global and regional, center and periphery, are much more complex today. As the Vietnamese filmmaker and writer Trin T. Minh-ha says, there are First Worlds in every Third World and Third Worlds in every First World, to say nothing of Second and Fourth Worlds. What does this complexity and contradiction do to the model of "critical regionalism," which again seems to rely on homogeneous local cultures for its articulation? How might it be complicated in its turn? And here, too, I think it should be developed, not rejected—that is my point. Perhaps it can be complicated along the lines of the model of "cognitive mapping" proposed by Frederic Jameson.[3] In this model Jameson relates the relative inability to map a phenomenological position in the megapolis—as demonstrated by Kevin Lynch and colleagues in the 1961 *The Image of the City*—to the relative inability to map international class relations in advanced capitalism. In so doing, he extrapolates the concept of cognitive mapping in Althusserian terms. And yet, though he complicates it greatly, the principle of a "map-in-the-head" seems to contradict his own diagnoses of the postmodern condition of schizoid subjectivities and deterritorialized spaces. This said, one can fully support the project—to think the renewal of sited political communities that can act locally and think globally.

If my discussion seems contradictory, it may well be. I am not sure of my own position among these discourses. And I know it is presumptuous to be critical of other programs and not to pose a program of my own. But I cannot. I can, however, point to a general problem that any contemporary critical practice must confront. This is not a problem strictly located "beyond" architecture; in fact, contemporary architecture sometimes addresses and sometimes abets it. The problem involves the principal ideologeme of the discourse of postmodernism: the atrophy of the historical sense and of the utopian imagination; more precisely, the inability to grasp the past except scenographically as a series of pictures or tableaux and to project the future except (again) in terms of entropy or apocalypse, according to scenarios of slow capitalist contamination or sudden technological catastrophe. Obviously, this inability circumscribes any practice that seeks to develop the contradictions of the present into a critical consciousness of past formations and future possibilities. In the space remaining, I want to touch on a few of its implications. I have discussed the problem of the future seen in terms of an autonomous technology in another place.[4] Here I want to focus on the problem of the past seen as a picture. Though invalidated a long time ago, this model remains operative in many ways.

We tend to cherish our faculty of memory even as its activity remains obscure to us. Yet, its institutional determinations are historically problematic. In antiquity, for example, memory was an aspect of rhetoric, part of a system of persuasion and power; in scholasticism, memory was an aspect of ethics, part of regimen of obedience and order. Of specific interest here is that from its institutional beginnings memory was often conceived in architectural terms as a mnemonic of place and image: in rhetoric the orator would devise an architecture of elements to which were assigned specific ideas, even words, to be recalled in the course of argument.[5] Now this particular art of memory may seem innocuous, but it sets up a persistent cultural pattern that is not innocuous: the tendency to think of memory in terms of space, in effect to spatialize time, to pictorialize history (which is probably part of a greater patriarchal privilege-granted vision). This has many ramifications: our tendency to consider knowledge in terms of visual sites (like topics, tables, taxonomies); more importantly, our tendency to reduce the past (personal and collective) to so many tableaux for aesthetic contemplation, which, as we know, is so often melancholic, nostalgic, passive. It is in this way, in part, that we restrict our historical apprehension, that we effectively repress many histories by our symptomatic representation of a few dominant ones. This, of course, is an old Freudian problem. In a famous early passage in *The Interpretation of Dreams*, Freud relates the dream to the rebus in order to suggest the folly of a pictorial reading as opposed to a linguistic interpretation. And in a famous late passage in *Civilization and its Discontents*, he suggests that it is misbegotten to see the individual unconscious in terms of space. There he draws the analogy of a ruinous Rome—of a Rome whose levels and fragments obscure one another. But the unconscious, he argues, does not work in this way; it is formed in a process of repression, not ruination. The same is true of our collective unconsciousness, of our tribal histories—or so I would argue. They cannot be spatialized, they should not be pictorialized. And yet this is how, at many levels of historical awareness, we still grasp the past—as a sequence of pictures, a series of monuments.

There is a painting in which this ideology is stated bluntly because confidently: *The Architect's Dream* (1840) by the American, Thomas Cole. There is much one might say about it. What, for example, is the mythical origin, the vanishing point, at which the architect gazes? Is this figure not, in some sense, a naive avatar of the *Angelus Novus* of Paul Klee and Walter Benjamin, who, caught up in the storm called progress that propels him backward into the future, sees nothing but ruins amass before him? Here, I invoke the painting simply as a diagram of the dynastic or imperial model of history. It is a model in which the architectural—the monumental—stands in for the historical. This fetishism of the monument serves two purposes—both to commemorate and to disavow historical change: to commemorate the ascendant (American) bourgeoisie as the self-proclaimed epitome of history, to commemorate its claim to a post-historical position from which history is simply collected as so many pictures or styles, and to disavow this history, to disavow that it, the bourgeoisie, is involved in historicity. Traditional art history is riven by this same contradictory ideology; architecture is, too. In fact, the still dominant model of art history—that of Wolfflin—tells its narrative as a continuous reinterpretation of past works, and this model is based—explicitly for Wolfflin—on the paradigm of architecture. It quickly became structural to the pedagogy of art history, especially when, with the technology of the photograph, the concept of transcendental style could be contrived and the method of abstract comparison established. To our eyes, the Cole painting might seem a parody before the fact of this art-historical model of opposed cyclical styles, but this is still dominant pedagogical practice. And that is my point, or rather my question: as crude, as obvious, as this ideology of the historicalness appears to us, I wonder if we have truly surpassed it. I do not mean simply its dynastic or linear aspects. I mean its fetishistic aspect, its selective-suppressive aspect. I mean the model of the past as picture, of history as stage (as in the Cole painting) and as rhetorical theater of exclusive memory performed strictly for us. For all the many critiques of historicism, most of us, I think, remain members of this modern cult of monuments.

Of course, my critique of the-past-as-picture is directed, in part, at so-called postmodern architecture, but it extends to many other practices as well. In two famous essays, "The Age of the World Picture" and "The Question Concerning Technology," Heidegger considered this problem. (His reflections on dwelling are also pertinent to my remarks on architecture and homelessness.) In the first essay, written before World War II, the-world-as-representation and the-individual-as-subject of-this-representation are seen to be coeval. In the second essay written after the war, both the-world-as-picture and the-individual-as-subjected-subject are seen to be produced out of a fundamental instrumentality that has become second nature to modern man. And here the crucial term is the past not only as picture but also, in this perspectival array, as "standing-reserve"—there as a repository to be used as we wish. This instrumentality is linked by Hiedegger to a pervasive technology, and it is this technology that he rails against (certainly his fascist sympathies are relevant here). Now, has architecture broken with any of this—with this model of the past as picture and standing-reserve, with this instrumentality and technology? Can it? If we want to develop a relationship to the past that is redemptive and not fetishistic, and a relationship to the future that is responsive and not destructive, I think it must. (There is also an historical question to ask in passing: What is the relation between the establishment of Architecture with a capital A and the instantiation of perspective? Was Architecture thus set up in perspectival opposition to the subject at its very beginning?)

By way of a conclusion, I want briefly to think about this problematic art of memory, this pictorial fetishism of history, as it is inscribed in our museum architecture and our museal culture in general. I want to do so by reference to a 1985 Louise Lawler photograph of a storage space in the Rude Museum in Dijon. (Rude is best known as the sculptor of the emblem of French nationalism, *La Marseillaise*, of 1833–36, part of a cast of which is seen in the center of the Lawler image.) The caption given to the photo reads in part: "The Art of Memory—the restriction and placement, its deposition in material form with extreme emphasis on presentation, selects a limited number of acceptable issues with limited ways to speak." Now this old art of memory lives on, of course, not only in architecture, but also in the museum. Indeed, the typical museum is a theater of memory where works of art as pictures of the past

The Rude Museum

serve fetishistically to occlude more than to clarify historical practices. But this theater of memory does not begin or end there. It is endemic to our museal culture: it may be one reason why we still tend to think time in terms of inert stages or phases rather than, say, dialectically or in difference. (Again, I would argue, architecture is emblematic of this history of periods and pictures.) This spatialization of time has an important corollary no less endemic to our museal culture: the tendency to temporalize space, so that different peoples are said to inhabit different times, so that "further away" comes to mean "more primitive." As Johannes Fabian argues in *Time and the Other: How Anthropology Makes Its Object* (1983), this is largely how we construct our others; if we do not deny them historical time altogether, we freeze them in the past. That is, either we assign them to different developmental moments in our own history, or we judge them according to an imposed criterion of authenticity whereby they only really existed—genuinely, purely—in the past. This pastoral myth of cultural loss seems sweet if sad, but its effects are insidious, for it positions other cultures as mere ruins that must be saved by us and stored in our own theaters of memory—in our texts, museums, architecture. This murderous myth not only permits the continued appropriation of the past of other cultures, but also blocks any constructive engagement with the "present-becoming-future" of these cultures.[6] In any case, one sees the effects not only of this pictorializing of our own past but also this plundering of other cultures everywhere in our culture today, and in many ways architecture has propounded this phantasmagoria more than any other cultural practice.

1. As the last speaker, I included in my talk a few remarks about the other papers, which I reproduce here as a set of impressions of the event as a whole.

As Walter Benjamin once wrote, the just-past can be a strong anti-aphrodisiac, and, generationally at least, we are involved in a certain Oedipal relationship with the addressed architects. Hence, perhaps, the ambivalent criticality of the papers. For example, Peggy Deamer, though sympathetic to the work of Michael Graves, wanted to see in its humanist solicitation of the viewer a paradoxical effacement of this subject. And Michael Hays, though intrigued by the work of Peter Eisenman, argued that its very reflexivity had led it to reflect the anomie of a fragmentary society. And though more sanguine, both Alan Plattus and Carol Burns suggested (at least to me) certain contradictions in the work of Venturi, Rauch and Scott Brown and Frank Gehry—contradictions between positions of populism and patronization; contradictions, especially in the case of Gehry, between the ideal of the commonplace and the ideology of artistic sublimation (whereby the architect redeems materials of low culture with no real change in the position or value of these terms).

These are all important insights, so why was I somewhat disappointed? Because we accepted the institutional frame of our own discussion. We delved critically into architectural conventions—but not into our own conceptual closures. We accepted the utter conventionality of a discussion centered on proper names, of a discourse of patronymic style: Graves, Johnson, Pelli, Roche, Pedersohn, Pei, Eisenman, Gehry . . . and we accepted the obvious ideology of the avant-garde—though it is institutional as cultural concept and social formation. Why is this so? Why is it difficult to think through these ideological limits, these disciplinary boundaries?

2. Kenneth Frampton, "Toward a Critical Regionalism: Six Points for an Architecture of Resistance," in Hal Foster, ed., *The Anti-Aesthetic: Essays on Postmodern Culture* (Seattle: Bay Press, 1983).

3. Frederic Jameson, "Cognitive Mapping," in C. Nelson and L. Grossberg, eds., *Marxism and the Interpretation of Cultures* (Urbana and Chicago: University of Illinois Press, 1988).

4. Hal Foster, "Neofuturism: Architecture and Technology," in *A.A. Files*, 14, (London: Architectural Association, Spring 1987).

5. Frances Yates, *The Art of Memory*.

6. I borrow this term from James Clifford, *The Predicament of Culture* (Cambridge: Harvard University Press, 1988), also his contribution in Hal Foster, ed., *Discussions in Contemporary Culture* (Dia Art Foundation/Bay Press, 1987).

THINKING THE PRESENT
DISCUSSION

JORGE SILVETTI: My role here is that of advancing the discussion, although with the amount of information presented in the last two days, I'm not sure I can advance it any further. Nevertheless, I would like to make a few points that may help move toward a discussion. First, I would like to reiterate Rafael Moneo's warning that no conclusions should be expected from such a symposium.

I think these two days have helped open all kinds of avenues of inquiry and at some points have dispersed, even dangerously, certain interests in analyzing architecture today. Following Rafael Moneo's comment yesterday on the format and the content of this conference, I would like to say again that there are certainly other ways this material we've been analyzing could be arranged and discussed. This symposium does not intend, by any means, to say that this is the way to look at these architects and their work, that this is the way to look at the architecture of the last twelve years, or that these last twelve years can be expected to explain the present. Maybe this conference is the beginning of other conferences by other institutions that would cut across all this information and all this history with a different perspective.

I recently attended a very, very different type of conference in Japan. Some Harvard faculty members were invited to talk about the current American city, and some of the very same slides appeared in the conference, and yet what we were talking about was something totally different. Perhaps we were not concerned at that conference about the present state of capitalism because we were talking with the Lash Corporation. Yet, I must say we were with a very unlikely group of people, unlikely because we usually talk only to architects rather than politicians and economists. I found that discussions about the problems of taxation and interest structures in American cities today, problems I continue to tackle as an architect, gave me as much information and as much enthusiasm as these last two days have, and, as I say, it was pretty much the same material that we were looking at.

Certainly one could look at these last twelve years in terms of the institutions that have advanced the ideas that architecture has realized: the schools of architecture; certainly the Institute of Architecture and Urban Studies in New York, which played a central role in developing and disseminating these ideas that we've been discussing; and the institutions of journalism and the press. Particularly interesting for me would be another conference that looks at the same type of material in terms of the vicissitudes of theory in architecture over the last fifteen years or so, because it seems to me that what we've been looking at is directly tied to the developments of theory and the appearance of the very phenomenon of architectural theory as we know it today.

I say this because I think that we need to reassess where we are in relation to theory, and I think these past two days have proved that. My observation is that we have been led to a kind of estrangement in how architecture is positioned relative to the rest of society. I think that the theory we have been practicing, and I am very self-critical about it, has led us to an inability to recognize architecture as a social practice that has changed drastically and is positioned very differently than it was even twelve years ago. We have been looking inward too much to the structure of architecture and architectural production. This has been very enlightening, but maybe it is time now to look outward and to see how those boundaries between architecture and other practices in society need to be redefined or staked out in a different way.

I have questions that emerged during these two days, and I don't want to force anybody to answer, but I would like the discussants to think about them. These questions have to do with those relationships between architecture and all the other social practices, in particular three practices with which architecture finds itself in a lamentable relationship. I will call them the three lamentable states of architecture.

First is architecture's relationship with art, a relationship of confusion. The presentation of Herbert Muschamp today was quite extraordinary because of the range of examples he gave about the "splinter practices" as he called them (which I liked very much). We must recognize they exist and we must explore them for their possible relationship with architecture. We are dealing with an incredibly heterogeneous field of things that are being done in the name of architecture. All of them have the right to exist and all of them influence each other, but we cannot ask that all of these things converge at the same time and in the same object. In fact, there seems to be emerging, in the last twenty years or so (parallel to all of these developments), a kind of independent practice, an artistic practice that figuratively represents and criticizes the institution of architecture through another medium. It is important to sort this practice out, to recognize that it exists, to identify its relationship with architecture, to put it in the proper place, and not to confuse it with the production of buildings.

The second lamentable state of architecture is a subservience to the institutions, if we may call them such, of scholarship and research. One of the prices we pay today in theory is the dependence on the importation of so many models from other disciplines. This is the result, perhaps, of the positive intensity of the work that has been done in academia in the last twenty years. But by borrowing from either history, philosophy, or, more heavily in the last few years, literary criticism, academia has denied architecture the ability to find its own research models.

The final lamentable state of architecture is that of ignorance in relation to the changes of the power structure in American society today. I must say that, for all the brilliance and attraction of Hal Foster's argument, I found it precisely and paradoxically detached from the reality of the relationships that architecture has with society, with power, and with the very people Foster feels should be included. We can ask Michael Graves how the Whitney is doing after its third community design review in order to understand the ways architecture in America, probably more than in any country, is engaged in a dialogue with the public. The answers may not be as positive as one wishes. In fact, it may be that the dialogue with the public is one of the forces that has made architecture compromise more and more, and it may be that liberation must come first from the people. There are only so many things one can ask architects and architecture to do.

These three general areas of concern have emerged, in my view, from what we have been looking at in this conference. I would now ask the panelists to address whatever other subjects they would like, and to think about the subject of the conference, "thinking the present."

MICHAEL GRAVES: The point was made over lunch that this conference was more about critical evaluation than about the work, which is probably true. I was surprised, in many of the presentations, that things I thought I knew were different from what was said, but I guess that is fair. That is what makes ball games. I was especially surprised in my own case to be called utopian. I thought I never had been such, and I am surprised that my work has been read that way by Peggy Deamer. I was probably hallucinating.

I think it was Herbert Muschamp, or maybe Hal Foster, who said there was a strong Oedipal thing going on. Peter and I have discussed this for ten years. He said that the generation represented by the speakers here hasn't fulfilled his aspirations, and I said, "You see, Peter, they are getting back at us." I still think that is partly true. What Peggy Deamer did in the first three quarters or more of her talk, I think, was extremely well done in terms of a very careful critical, analysis of the early work, but when she got to the last twelve years, of course, the work was dismissed summarily, using words, phrases, and ideas that were on a very different plane than the earlier evaluation. I was surprised that there was something there that got in the way. I would like to have a conversation with her about what I did twelve years ago that upset her. I have always thought that Peter's architecture was pessimistic and mine, not utopian, but optimistic. I have often teased Peter about wanting to be Norman Rockwell during the night and himself during the day. And in a way, I find his work very pessimistic during the day and his life very optimistic at night. What I find about myself is the reverse.

I was very surprised to see work credited to other people; that was an enormous surprise to me. There is a phrase from Le Corbusier, where he comments on engineers as having "eyes that do not see." Perhaps critics have eyes that see too much. I began to resist Herbert Muschamp's narrative at the point when I saw a rug shaped vaguely like Tennessee and heard his comments. It was read, and read for me in a way that precluded all the things that were supposed to be left open.

I was thinking to myself about my own last dozen years or so. In contrast to other folks here at the table, I was seen as the one who closes the question. How far off I must be because, though there was not much discussion of the city, I worry that I may preclude other variations on the city with regard to the traditional city. I feel owed by the critics at least a demonstration of how some of the work discussed—whether a floating cloud over the interstate, or Frank Gehry's work in Los Angeles, or Steven Holl's work in New York—translates ultimately in terms of the city, how those questions being left open by those architects and certainly by all of their critics finally add up to a place where we can do what we did an hour ago, that is, have lunch. I find myself so terribly old fashioned that, more and more, I do not belong in situations like this, as I struggle against the pessimism of lunch and continue to look for my cafe, I suppose. I know it is very out of place to suggest a kind of nostalgia for the city, but a long time ago I decided that looking at a piece of sculpture that was essentially rusting metal did not give me pleasure, and that the critical reading of it was so far fetched I needed something else. I suppose the last dozen years or so have been an attempt on my part to look for and try to imagine and identify those elements in what we do, in the com-

position of a building and in its relationships to the city and to other buildings. These relationships not only give pleasure but also make a connection to what I have found to be my reality and the reality of a number of
other people as well.

PEGGY DEAMER: In speaking of utopianism I wanted to emphasize what
I see as your sincere efforts to make our lives more pleasurable and more elevated and, perhaps, more sacred. In many ways, I admire that. In fact, that is
the essence of what I do admire in your work. But maybe the problem lies in
how one defines pleasure or, as you were saying, how one connects to your
reality, or how you expect others to define reality. I have no problem with
the idea of giving pleasure and connecting to reality, but in a way that will
make people conscious of things that are not only the easy and beautiful
things in their lives, but the more difficult things as well. To concern oneself
with the city is to introduce broader questions about making structures that
are not easily taken in and then dismissed because the pleasure was immediate
but not demanding.

MICHAEL GRAVES: Why do you think that is what I meant? That the
pleasure I was referring to was immediate and superficial?

PEGGY DEAMER: Perhaps because you brought up the issue of not finding pleasure in rusted steel. When I compare the work implied by that comment to images you present to us, I see a difference between your pleasure
and a more difficult pleasure, one that I might consider plausible.

MICHAEL GRAVES: Yes, today one honors difficulty in certain versions of
critical debate. It is a great rhetorical device. It yields a great distance from
many versions of pleasure. I suppose what I mean by rusting steel is that I
watched over the past twenty years buildings constructed that were meant to
be refrigerators in the landscape. And they are that the first day, but when left
out in the rain, they become something else. The problem is that there is no
"409" to clean them up daily. I am at ease with the idea that a building
changes, deteriorates, or is in some way embellished over time because of its
context, if that is the intention of its author. In many versions of what we see
today, that is not the intention.

PEGGY DEAMER: Perhaps you could talk about what I was proposing—
that the early work was very difficult. I think it was difficult for a person to
understand, be in, and feel confident in. In the present work that is not true.
I would like to hear you talk about whether you agree, and how you would
characterize the difference between then and what you present to people
now and how you would like them to react to it.

MICHAEL GRAVES: Peter and I proposed an article to one of the architectural magazines to get a debate going among architects At that time it was considered illegal by the AIA for one architect to discuss the work of another publicly. We proposed to the magazine that they have a "five on five." There were strong evaluations of the five architects by the five other people, whom we helped to choose and who were on "the other side" at that time. It was interesting that Charles Moore, in his evaluation of the Benaceraff House, felt he was a very good reader of language. But when the language used by the architect was so incredibly private that there were either too many options open or too few, when the language was so internalized that entrance into it by another was precluded, Moore was left outside. The last thing I wanted to do was to be private. All through the time I had been working, I felt that it was more interesting to speak both the common language of the man on the street and, at the same time, the language of the academy. If I were populist only, I would run the risk of missing the evaluation of my colleagues. I have always felt that both languages are possible. The last dozen years have been spent trying to embellish a language where there are many actors in the play.

DENISE SCOTT BROWN: Thinking the Present. If you take 1977 as the definitive date, what happened to us then was, at last, we got some work. When this happened, we became involved in the practice of architecture and in making our practice good. Since we have been busy, we have heard distant rumors of movements among the critics—de-this and re-that. When I come here I find I am, at one level, a fossil, and, at another, a working stiff; I don't understand this un-understandable discourse.

I wrote down a few phrases as I was listening, some for liking, some for not understanding. One, which stands for numerous statements in the critics's presentations that I did not understand, was Peggy Deamer's: "The representation of the threshold . . . is no longer obscure, even if 'missing.' " Another one I wrote down because I liked it and had a question: The office building is a paltry building type and not the receptacle of our greatest aspirations. We have never designed an office building because we have never had the opportunity to do so. Steven Holl is right that the office building is not the receptacle of our greatest aspirations, but maybe it should be designed in a way to show that it is not. This does not mean that one should not design an office building, but maybe offices should not be designed to look like civic monuments.

Another comment I found moving was Alan Plattus's interpretation of civic humanism—provisional humanistic engagement with traditional civic values, as in the Italian Renaissance or as Aalto did it. For me, architectural monumentality is acceptable when it is a provisional humanistic engagement with civic values, when it derives (perhaps not easily) from its society. A building may claw its way to grandeur, or search its way to grandeur, but certainly not posture its way to grandeur. Grandeur can come out of something good; this seems to be the answer to the comment about paltry aspirations.

For all that, I agreed with Hal Foster on the need to connect social issues with architecture. It is something I thought I had been trying to do for the last twenty years. One of my complaints with the critics is that they never notice. When critics come to the office they look at built works. They hardly glance at projects. They certainly don't want to see my urban plans and designs. A study on Memphis came out of the office last year and sank without a trace. No one ever asked about it, except for a few Europeans who became very excited and wondered how I learned to do that kind of work; it was in part by studying urban economics, which Jorge Silvetti, too, feels is relevant.

Let me just add that it was a joy to hear Alan Plattus talk about our work. Every time he brought up a point, I wanted to add ten more, but of course, he wanted to add those ten, too. He did an excellent job of editing and his thesis on our work is one of the most interesting and is acceptable to us.

I would like to say that we are modernists, not postmodernists. No one is a postmodernist. Maybe postmodernism is dead. I feel our original concept, whether "mo" or "pomo," has been greatly misunderstood. When I hear that there is no social relevance to our work, that we sit on the lap of American wealth, that we are slime encrusted on the facades of Trafalger Square, I feel it unfortunate that the critics don't realize that much of our way of thinking derived from the social movements of the 1960s, and that the axes of influence on us extend across the Atlantic. Many of my ideas derive from my origins in Africa and my experience with new brutalism in England. Those connections are only now being made by critics. People now ask me what I knew about the Independent Group in London, but it is the first time in all these years that anyone has thought to ask. Although American critics do not know that these things are relevant influences on our work, I don't think it is possible to understand us without this knowledge. Nor will you understand unless you know what we learned from the social planners at the University of Pennsylvania, from the new left, and from the civil movements in America in the sixties, and how we reacted to them. At the same time we wrote *Learning from Las Vegas* we were advocate planners on South Street. Both strands have continued in our work, and you will find both in our designs for the National Gallery. But they will be hard to recognize if you feel such issues are not relevant to architecture.

ALAN PLATTUS: Both Michael Graves and Denise Scott Brown have
made comments about something that comes up in their otherwise very different work, something we perhaps did a very bad job with: The most important thing that has happened not only on the American scene but also the international scene in the last twelve years is coming to terms with the
phenomenon of the city as the place where we operate as architects. I think
that probably the format of the conference, which I do not want to criticize,
deflected some attention away from that. I think it is good to be reminded by
the people who listen to us that many of their concerns grew out of different
kinds of reflections on urbanism and the problems of the city.

JORGE SILVETTI: I am very happy that Denise Scott Brown, reflecting on
her own work and the origins of some of her thought, has tied the work to
the social concerns of the sixties. Indeed, what has been lost by the current
historians is that origin of most of the thought and theory of recent architecture. The origins of contemporary theory are based on certain interests in
present culture and begin as a criticism of the architecture of the time because of its social irrelevance. I can say that because, personally, that is when
the greatest change came in my life—when I came to this country and heard
Robert Venturi and Denise Scott Brown speak in Berkeley where I was a student. It was that particular line of thought that produced some of the lines of
contemporary thinking. So the accusations today of formalism or social
relevance must be weighed against a foundation, and this must be solid.

PETER EISENMAN: I thought I was going to reply to the critics, but I
think I have to do so quickly because I feel impingements from the left and
the right and I would like to reply briefly to Michael Graves and Denise
Scott Brown. I always love it when Michael tries to put me in a pessimistic
box. It fills me with a kind of wonderment. I am always amazed when Denise—
and it is Denise, not Robert Venturi, because Robert never comes to these
things. He is always too busy. He was always too busy, even when he didn't
have any work, to engage in any debate. He set up the debate and then
refused to play. And then, when they complain about critics not treating them
fairly, it is perhaps because the critics are tired of the fact that they don't want
to play. As one of the only people who has written about this period and set
up the period, Robert has the responsibility to come and not try to send a sur-
rogate. [Boos from the audience.] I have never had the chance to face him. I
always end up facing you. I like you. I have no problem with you. I just want
to know why, since Robert walked out of a Case meeting in 1963, and since
Michael and I have tried to engage Robert Venturi in debate, he has never
shown up.

I would like to address my remarks to Mr. Filler and Mr. Muschamp. Since I
was not featured in either of their talks, I therefore cannot be accused of wor-

rying about the critique of my own practice. I find that they set the tone for this discussion, and I find it a rather dismal tone.

Filler takes the so-called six professional offices and gratuitously, as far as I am concerned, attacks them. Why were they singled out? I never understood the grounds for the criticism. Everybody is open to criticism, but you have to define the grounds. I don't blame Cesar Pelli and David Childs for not wanting to participate in their own frying. It would be crazy for them to do that. What is interesting about Mr. Filler is that he earns his living by propagating big time-stuff through *House & Garden*, and I wonder why he is beating on the people who keep him in business.

While Mr. Filler is reviling the center, Mr. Muschamp is glorifying the fringe. He starts with the traditional, left wing, social, knee-jerk response to Gordon Matta-Clark. Matta-Clark once came into my Institute, which was a place of debate, with a loaded twenty-two caliber rifle and shot out the windows. To me that was a very aggressive act. He said he was only doing it for art. It is very easy to chop up buildings and call it a critique of society, but it is no longer architecture. I think there are big differences between a criticism of society, sculpture, environmental art, fringe drawings, marginalia, et cetera, and architecture. I want to argue that of what Mr. Muschamp showed, very little was architecture. Very little of it was buildable or built or going to be built in the social framework of society. When he shows built work, I say, "Is that what he means?" He shows us these office-building interiors done by Billie Tsien and Tod Williams, but if that is what Muschamp means by getting it right in the built environment, I want to go home.

We have to realize there is a big difference between drawing and building. I do agree with Denise that it is very difficult to build. The critics get very upset when people who are interested in theory, like Venturi and Scott Brown, Michael Graves, and myself, begin to build and build a lot. They say, "Oh my god, there is a change, there is no longer a theoretical charge in the work." I maintain that it is enormously difficult to build, but to build ideas is even more difficult. And I would like to challenge any of the critics to go see any of my built work and say that there is not a charge in them.

I think, in conclusion, that I don't mind anything critics say because I believe that the artist-architect is the last person to know what he or she thinks about what he or she is doing. It is not the obligation of the artist or architect to necessarily be knowing at all stages of the work. You can reflect on work. Therefore, I find in enormously stimulating to hear what Michael Hays has to say about what I want to do. I wonder, had she been subjected to the same kind of criticism that Michael Graves and I had been subjected to, if Denise would have been so happy with Alan Plattus.

HERBERT MUSCHAMP: I think it very exciting when architects who are known primarily through theoretical work and through drawing and writing enter a phase in their career when they become more actively engaged in building. It is very exciting to see you in that phase. I see one of my functions as a critic is to support people when they are not at the stage you are. I see that as one of my responsibilities. I am not as interested as firmly as you are in drawing boundaries about whether it is architecture or not.

MARTIN FILLER: I will leave it to Peter Eisenman to lower the tone of the debate in his inimitable fashion. The *ad hominem* remarks about my presentation, the *ad feminem* nature of his comments to Denise Scott Brown, are certainly in his preferred mode of trying to toss marbles beneath the feet of the dancers. I would just like to remind him that *House & Garden* presented his House Six (the Frank House) in 1978, only six months after its publication in *Progressive Architecture*. In the current issue of the magazine I have written about a house by his recent partner, Jack Robertson, and later this year we will be publishing Peter's new loft in New York. Almost never have the pages of *House & Garden* featured the work of the large commercial firms shown in my talk yesterday. To attempt to answer his disingenuous question—"What have those firms done wrong?"—I think the visual material I showed largely spoke for itself. The enormously destructive impact that those schemes have had on our urban environment virtually requires no further comment. Neither does the mock shock with which he reacted to my "frying" of those firms, though there were also a number of positive comments that I made. The only possible explanation for his response is that Peter's debt to his *padrone*, Philip Johnson, required this public defense of what I see as indefensible work.

PETER EISENMAN: If you think your presentation and some of the others were of such a high level that I demean them, then I apologize. But I don't believe that the discourse was at that high a level.

RAFAEL MONEO: I disagree with the tone that has been established, Peter. I disagree because it seems to me to misconstrue, in a way, the intentions of the conference. I am not going to comment about the pertinence of Martin Filler's presentation on the large firms. What is still interesting is how, after the change of aesthetic aspirations in the seventies, those firms follow almost like a herd, giving up completely those stylistic modes practiced before. To examine how the formal mechanisms that have been explored and discussed in the schools evolved into the hands of those firms—producing, at the end, a body of work I wouldn't dare say is always satisfactory—is, in my view, an attractive subject. Because, indeed, it has not been very much explored how the language and the rules established in the schools were "instrumentalized" by the big firms, affecting the appearance of American cities. It has not been examined either how these changes are related to the sociopolitical American atmosphere in the last few years.

I think that your reply to Martin Filler displaces to personal grounds the interests and intentions of the conference. Instead, I would like to give an answer to the more general questions just raised. To connect Michael Graves's change and its impact on the big firms is still an interesting page to be written in the modern history of architecture. It would explain what history and style mean for those architects who have established the image and the face of American cities in the late seventies and early eighties. I liked Muschamp's intervention, exploring the fringes. I don't agree with the idea of architecture that is expressed in many of the examples that he presented, but at the same time, it seems to me that it is quite important to admit the broad set of dispersed circumstances that claim to be related in one way or another with architecture. We try to explain at the school what the ground of the discipline is, but also try to pay respect to those marginal and fringe attempts to create other architectures. This is necessary if we consider the school as being concerned with research and knowledge.

JORGE SILVETTI: I would like to ask Alan Colquhoun to come forward. We have discussed some of the issues of this conference with Alan, and, as a critic from another generation than those who have presented here, his comments would be of interest.

ALAN COLQUHOUN: As I understand it, the symposium started off with the intention to give a rendering of the last twelve years or so as an account of where we are now. It has been more and less than this. It has been less in the sense that such a survey is bound to be very selective and to filter out, necessarily and from the start, certain works and boundaries. It has been more because what has been under scrutiny, perhaps more than the architectural works being discussed, is the number of critical discourses that have been going on, overlapping, diverging, contradicting, and passing over each others's heads.

I just want to mention two directions that seem contradictory to each other, which is in itself interesting. There were those critics like Alan Plattus and Carol Burns who took a position, which I think is entirely justifiable, that sought to naturalize the objects of their study within an existing discourse— within that or a Rorty or a Vico—seen as a kind of opposition to a supposedly perennial and hegemonic rationalism. In other words, we have been presented with Venturi and Scott Brown and Frank Gehry as people who are part of the eternal reaction against rationalism, which is kind of public enemy number one but, at the same time, is always in a dominant position and cannot be dislodged. These presentations were examples of a discourse that is within the boundaries of, and generally supported by, the architects of the study.

The other type of critique is represented by those who placed themselves radically outside existing boundaries and who took a negative attitude towards existing architectural production. One couldn't say that Peggy Deamer's attitude towards Graves was quite like this since she was clearly operating within his own terms of reference when she was discussing his work of the late 1970s. But she did reject his work entirely after that, and one could say that she is operating outside present architectural practice in that respect.

The main example of this attempt to operate outside the boundaries is that of Michael Hays. Michael showed a supportive view of "negative" architecture and presented Peter as representing this negation. In advocating negativity, I think Michael found in the present cultural situation a subject that represented just this negativity. Therefore, Michael didn't—and I think it a pity—exercise his critical skills in discussing Eisenman's own critical practice. He attributed to Eisenman attitudes characteristic of his own discourse. Eisenman's work was seen, in Michael's terms, as making strange (in the Shklovskian sense of the word), as producing an alienation effect, as using strategies of appropriation, as assuming the death of the subject, and as taking an attitude of resistance towards existing and past structures. As interesting as I found his talk, it would have been even more interesting if he had questioned the relation between theory and practice in Eisenman's work, which I find to be problematic in some respects, and had then, perhaps, gone on to ask in what way is it possible to conceive of an architecture of negation, pure and simple. In this, I find myself in sympathy with Hal Foster in his call for an annunciatory criticism of affirmation. How can we be affirmative without accepting any existing aspects of society? This is one of the problems raised during this conference and which has certainly not been settled.

AUTHOR BIOGRAPHIES

PEGGY DEAMER is an assistant professor of architecture at Columbia University and a principal in the New York firm of Deamer and Phillips. She has a Bachelor of Architecture from Cooper Union. At Princeton University, Deamer completed a Master and Doctorate in Architecture, doing thesis research on the English art critic Adrian Stokes and serving as associate editor for the first Princeton Journal, *Ritual*.

MARTIN FILLER is a critic and writer, a former associate editor at *Progressive Architecture* and currently an editor of *House and Garden*. Educated at Columbia University with a Masters degree in Art History, Filler has published widely on design, architecture, and art. His work includes research on the social history of the American country house, the interior landscape and the politics of change, and American architecture and criticism.

ALAN PLATTUS is an associate professor of architecture at Yale University. He is also a practicing architect and is currently working on a design for Flushing Meadows in New York City. After studying at Yale University, he earned a Masters degree in Architecture at Princeton University. Plattus has since taught at Princeton, Catholic University, University of Miami, and University of Pennsylvania. He has lectured throughout the United States on contemporary criticism and is working on a book about civic pageantry.

K. MICHAEL HAYS is an assistant professor of architecture at the Harvard GSD, teaching seminars in theory and criticism as well as design studios. He is the founding editor of the architectural journal *Assemblage*. He received a Master of Architecture from MIT, where he is currently completing his doctoral dissertation. Hays has taught at Princeton University and Rhode Island School of Design. He has written on ideological issues of the European avant-garde and on current debates in the field of critical theory.

CAROL BURNS is an assistant professor of architecture at Harvard, teaching design studios and seminars on contemporary topics. As an architect, she has established her own practice with projects in Connecticut and Massachusetts. Burns has a Master of Architecture from Yale, where she edited the journal *Perspecta* and organized a project of site-specific constructions by architects and sculptors. She has taught at the University of Cincinnati and Rhode Island School of Design.

HERBERT MUSCHAMP is an architecture critic for the *New Republic* and *Artforum*. He developed and continues to direct the Graduate Program in Architecture and Design Criticism at Parson School of Design. He was educated at the University of Pennsylvania, Parsons, and the Architectural Association. Muschamp has contributed actively to many publications, including *The New Yorker* and *Vogue*. He is the author of two books, *File Under Architecture* and *Man About Town*, published by MIT Press.

HAL FOSTER is a critic of art, architecture, and culture, and is currently an art history instructor at the Whitney Independent Study Program. He cofounded the journal *Zone* and has been senior editor of *Art in America*. Foster has edited several books including *The Anti-Aesthetic: Essays in Post Modern Culture* and two Dia Foundation books. His own book of collected essays is called *Recodings*.